# HOW TO TAKE A SELFIE

A Motivational Workbook on Loving Yourself, Spiritual Healing And How To Get Your Life

Simone T. Allen

November Media Publishing, Chicago IL.
Copyright © 2018 Simone T. Allen

All rights reserved. No part of this publication may be reproduced, distributed, or transmitted in any form or by any means, including photocopying, recording, or other electronic or mechanical methods, without the prior written permission of the publisher, except in the case of brief quotations embodied in critical reviews and certain other noncommercial uses permitted by copyright law. For permission requests, write to the publisher, addressed "Attention: Permissions Coordinator,"
at the email address below.

November Media
info@novembermediapublishing.com

Ordering Information: Special discounts are available on quantity purchases by corporations, associations, and others. For details, contact the publisher at the email address above.
Printed in the United States of America

Produced & Published By November Media Publishing
ISBN: 978-0-9990431-4-1 (Print)

First Edition : January 2018

10 9 8 7 6 5 4 3 2 1

This book is dedicated to my heavenly Father. I honestly could have not wrote this without you.

I also dedicate this book to my two children Jeremiah and Nyimah. Always follow God plans for you. Never be afraid to follow your dreams.

# Contents

Prologue

Chapter 1:
## The Test

Chapter 2:
## Call the Doc

Chapter 3:
## Change Your Lifestyle

Chapter 4:
## Finding the Sex

Chapter 5:
## Your Name

Chapter 6:
## The Nesting Stage

Chapter 7:
## The Water Breaks

Original Poem by Simone Star
## Who Child is This?

*Thank you*

## *A note from the author...*

*"Our walk with the Lord is about a person named Jesus Christ."*
–Elder Shanel King

**Step one:** Understand that you are already amazing. Have you considered this before? Seriously, everything about you is totally epic. Including the part that needs some work. During our time together, I want you to get real with yourself. Like, no make-up real. In order for this to truly work, you have to bare your soul to the Lord. If you hide pieces of yourself, you're wasting your time. He wants every little bit of you. Only then can true change happen.

**Step two:** This is not a simple book, and I am not going to coddle you. It's important to understand this early on. However, it is a workbook meaning you need to put in the work for it to be effective. God loves you, but you must work to get better. He isn't a fairy godmother. No bibbity bobbity boo here pumpkin (see what I did there?). All jokes aside, if you are truly ready to accept your TRUE identity in Christ, carry on. If not, thank you. Come again when you're ready to work.

**Step three:** Take a deep breath and understand the first thing you need to do is let go of whatever plan you have for your life. Not to say that plans do not work, but they are pointless if they do not match up with the plan God has for you (Jeremiah 29:11). Your life will NEVER be perfect. Nothing can or will change this. Embrace this fact, and wear it well. Some people go through life trying to reach goals that are unattainable. Perfection doesn't exist except in God Himself.

I hope you enjoy our time together. Furthermore, I hope you're bursting with excitement at the thought of becoming who you were destined to be. To keep it simple, please note there won't be a lot of steps in this book. Mainly because I do not care for formality lol #nolie. I move like water, creating my own path rather than following the easier one. Most entrepreneurs do! It seems like I'm a narcissist, right? So far, this book has included a lot of I's and not too many yours. Perhaps this is due to the fact that I want to be as transparent with you as possible. There will be no holding back. Joy, tears, and laughter will be shared. Understand that I am your friend, and by sharing many horrid stories of my personal life, you will be better and do better. Now, let's get started.

# *Prologue*

*"Satan attacks your identity from birth"*
—Simone T. Allen

Remember, the title of the book is How to Take A Selfie. A Selfie is the way one takes a picture of oneself by using the front camera on their device. I've noticed there are some people who are incapable of taking a selfie. Not because they don't know how, but because it makes them uncomfortable. Now, for those of you who completely love yourself and always have, this may be a hard concept for you to understand. Please note that not everyone loves themselves. In fact, a large percentage of people actually have a hard time accepting and loving themselves. Most of which are reading this book. I saw on the Wendy Williams Show (how you doing), that women only look in the mirror to make sure everything is ok, verses men, who look because they admire their faces. Geesh, that sucks. I remember when I was much like the women who took the poll, avoiding the mirror whenever possible. As if a look in it would surely confirm my most in-depth thought of my lack of beauty. Currently, I am like the men in the poll; I look to admire more than anything. It didn't happen overnight. It has been an intense journey that I am still on.

Growing up in Chicago (before my two youngest sisters were born), there were only three of us. My eldest sister and the sister right under me. My oldest sister Chiquista has high yellow complexion. She is drop dead gorgeous and extremely charismatic. I watch people swoon over her all the time while she is completely unaware. Quita has always been in shape, but if you ask her, she'll tell you something different. As women, we never seem to give ourselves enough credit. Any who that woman slays. My younger, whom we refer to as Baby has a light caramel complexion and the biggest megawatt smile ever! Being the youngest, she honed on that "baby cute" skill early. Baby has also been the fit sister for the most part. Honestly, growing up that drove me crazy because Baby never had to watch what she ate. That woman takes no prisoners and I love it.

## Simone Allen

Now, smack dead in the middle of these two naturally beautiful women was me; the darkest of the three, with a natural brown complexion and chubby. Gracefully, there is the lovely term thick, which has been widely accepted. I was thick before people knew what thick was. Any who, I stood out compared to my sisters, and people never ceased to remind me of it. From my skin color, to my size, my extremely thick coarse hair and nerdy tendencies, I was dubbed the less than cute one. I never had a nickname because my name was as simple as pie (which is my birthday 3/14) Simone, yet people had a hard time remembering it. Instead, they referred to me as the big one, the dark one, the nerdy one, etc. You get the point. I always felt the need to defend myself since I didn't engage in the world around me too much. I would tell myself "Simone your size is the perfect size for you (hey, mamma made these hips), your honey kissed skin is beautiful and your mane resembles that of royalty in the animal kingdom, the Lion." This is before natural hair was popular so my type of hair (course and kinky) caused a fuss amongst the women in my life. It was a consistent reminder that I didn't' fit in with the rest of my family and they had no clue what to do with me. Nevertheless, the negative comments continued in my life, and I believed every word that was said about me.

The kids at school were pretty vicious and didn't make life any easier for me. I stood out and they made sure that I knew it. Now, this isn't like a movie. No one pulled my hair or laid a hand on me, pushed me in a locker or anything like that; but they didn't want anything to do with me either. Often, hurtful things were said behind my back and sometimes to my face. It would always come back to me through people who were associates. I never understood why they gave me a hard time when I stayed pretty much to myself. As you grow in life, you began to understand the world a bit more. Bullies tend to have been bullied themselves. They also have a very strong desire to fit in. I've also grown to understand that people shy away from what they don't understand. "To each its own," I would tell myself because it hurt being the outsider. There was no one in my life to tell me I was perfect the way I was, no one to say, "Simone you're beautiful," and so I never knew that I had such a power. That if I loved myself, truly loved me, then nothing else mattered. I definitely did not know the power of God's love. Love was a thing I only saw in the movies. It's not to say I wasn't loved by my family, but it wasn't something that was said out loud. I have learned this was true with a lot of families. We never say what we need to say. Based on my experiences, I thought I knew exactly what love was. However, my misinterpretation of love would have me seeking for love in all the wrong places.

Before we continue and get deeper into my past, I want you to do an exercise. Grab your phone, and take a selfie. Don't add anything or take off anything. Take a selfie as you are right now. You need to know that you will be doing a lot of this while reading this book. In fact, you are going to take a selfie every day for a year. Don't fuss; we will get to that selfie challenge later on in the book.

As you can see, I had no idea who I was. Christ tells us that we are all someone. "I am chosen." (1Thessalonians 1:4 NIV). He actually tells us this multiple time in the Bible. Why is identity so important? Why does any of this matter? Well here's why: If you do not know who you are, then you are subject to believe who people say you are. Total identity crisis! I'm sure you don't want a Melissa McCarty's character running around buying massage chairs in your name. Besides the financial reasons, knowing your identity also helps you discover your calling. The wrong identity can and will set you on the wrong path. (Jeremiah 29:11).

Everything that I went through in the beginning had to do with my identity. Honestly, my unpleasant childhood experience was the beginning of the attack on my identity. You see, Satan started his attack while I was still in the womb. When I think about it deeper, it probably started as soon as God decided to create me. Growing up, I felt like I didn't have a voice. During those tough school days, I had stopped talking for long periods of times. I became shy, which eventually turned into self-hatred. I also became guarded and wouldn't let people in. I felt that I had nothing worthy to say and that nobody would listen to me. Yet, this is the exact opposite of what the Lord says about me. In fact, it is through speech and my unique sound that the Lord has used to me to fish. Do you see how sneaky and conniving the enemy is? The torment, outcast and muteness were what the enemy wanted me to believe. Direct opposite of the authority platform and creative speaking abilities the Lord put in me. This isn't true just for me but for us all. Wherever the enemy is attacking you is where your identity lies.

Time for another exercise, loves. Do you know your identity? If so, write it down and thank the Lord for his grace upon your life. If not, look up scriptures and pray to the Holy Spirit for guidance. Our Father doesn't withhold information from us. Trust me, he is thrilled to share this with you. Think about your life, starting with your birth. Concentrate on the areas that caused you the most pain. For example, I became reserved but I am anointed to speak. Where has Satan attacked you at the most? Here are a few scriptures that helped me discover my identity. "I am the apple of my Father's eye?" (Psalm 17:8 NIV). "I am loved with an everlasting love." (Jeremiah 31:3 NIV). The people around you also play a potent role in discovering your identity. Do you have spiritual leaders? If so, write down their names. If not, again, ask the Holy Spirit to lead you to them. This person does not have to be a family member or a leader in your church. Your spiritual leaders will intercede on your behalf, help you figure out messages from the Lord and help you stay on track. Do not confuse the role of your spiritual leader with God; they are not Jesus nor the Holy Spirit, but a tool the Lord uses to help you throughout your life. Remember, they too are human; do not place them on a pedestal.

How to Take a Selfie

When I first moved to Virginia, I was very lost. I was raised in a church for most of my life, but I did not have a strong relationship with God. Honestly, before I moved to Virginia I wasn't even aware that you could have a relationship with Him. In my mind, He was this person who said He loved me, but I couldn't feel it. I grew up in fear of this omnipotent God who I assumed was judgmental and must have hated me to create me as so different, weird, nerdy, cool and with a mind that comprehends things a lot different than most. As you can see, I didn't know Him or myself. As a very reserved person I struggled to let people in. This was mostly due to the fact of how much I observed people's behaviors. I noticed that people would say one thing and do another. I trusted no one. I also didn't take advice from those who were trying to help me. It felt like it was me against the world.

One day, during service at my new church in Hampton, VA (Cornerstone International Worship Center), our Pastor called those who were broken to the alter for prayer. I felt a strong urge to go. I tried to resist the urge. I didn't want to be in front of the entire congregation. Fear and the enemy tried to convince me that they would judge me. Finally, I gave in to the guidance of the Holy Spirit and went up. When I did, a woman prayed for me. Almost instantly, I felt a strong connection to her, and was able to let my guard down a bit. At least enough for me to allow for her to lay hands on me for prayer. If you haven't already been able to tell, I was totally social awkward and had a "don't touch" policy. During prayer, God began to speak to me through this woman. I was shocked. God speaks through the people of today? Sure, I had heard the stories of Moses, but I don't think I truly understood it until then. After she was done praying for me, I felt a bit relieved. God does hear me! Today I am so grateful I humbled myself and let the Holy Spirit lead me. That wonderful woman of God is currently one of my spiritual leaders. God has used them to help me get a deeper understanding of my identity. She, along with my other spiritual leaders, prayed for me when I didn't even know how. God has truly blessed me with people who care for my well-being. Do you know who your spiritual leaders are? You should feel a divine connection to those called to be in your life. The Lord will make it apparent; He is not the Lord of confusion.

## How to Take a Selfie

You are wonderful! Often, we seek validation from others to satisfy the need to fit in. However, you are not like others. There is no one else like you. You are wonderfully made in His image Psalms 139:14 "I praise you because I am fearfully and wonderfully made; your works are wonderful, I know that full well. Did you know you have the power to validate yourself? You don't believe me, right? You are probably making a face, giving me side eye or shaking your head in disagreement. Am I right? The truth still stands: you are WONDERFUL. There is NO one like you. It doesn't matter if you look like someone else. They are NOT you, and you are NOT them. Each and every one of us have our own gifts, personality, and more important our own spirit. You can share DNA but you can NOT share a spirit. Truthfully, we waste so much time comparing ourselves to others, and often we degrade ourselves for not being like someone else. Stop it. It's not healthy, and it is not fair to you or the person you're comparing yourself to.

Exercise time. You guys are going to be super fit when you are done with this book due to all the exercising you're doing and what not. I see you flexing those self-love muscles. Oh wee, you guys look good! Stand in a mirror and tell yourself the following: I look good, I am victorious, there is no one like me, I am His masterpiece and I am wonderfully made in His image. I want you to say it at least 5 times. Each time I want you to say it louder and louder. Shout it as loudly as possible because it's true, you're a rock star.

As life continues, you are going to be faced with storms that make you feel otherwise. If you believe great things about yourself, then you will be able to weather any storm or any negativity the world throws to you. More importantly, if you learn to walk by faith and not by sight (2 Corinthians 5:7), then you'll learn how to become unstoppable because of the Lord. There is a great quote I have on my living room wall. It states "Life isn't about waiting for the storm to pass. It's about learning to dance in the rain." (Vivian Greene). You have to know that storms will always come, but they will always pass too. Let's not forget that every storm has a rainbow. You won't be in the storm forever and you are not alone. God is always with us. A great motivational song that you can listen to is "Lay It Down" by Sanctus Real. Absolutely amazing. This song continues to help me push through. I highly encourage you to listen to it and read the lyrics. As

## How to Take a Selfie

a matter of fact, do it now. Google it, let it play, read the lyrics, and let it marinate your soul. Yes child, let it sink in deep. Oh, don't forget to enjoy it and dance. I'm a firm believer in dancing stress off. Get silly, let loose and enjoy your life!

# I Pledge

to try when I want to quit. To cry, scream and shout if I need to. To trust God even when my flesh doesn't want to. I pledge to run after my dreams and to explore the uncharted. To grow even when it hurts. I pledge to embrace my future and learn from my past. To be all that God has called me to be. I pledge to be ME! Uniquely ever loving rock star, Me. To dance around, laugh until my cheeks are red and eat snacks I have no business eating. I pledge to shift the world and others around me by informing them of you. To lean on you in all times and with all things. I pledge to worship you. But most importantly I pledge to be a representation of you my Heavenly Father in all things. In Jesus nameAmen#letsdothis #werock

Chapter 1

# The Test: Congrats, You're Having a Baby!

*"I am God's child for I am born again of the incorruptible seed of the Word of God which lives and abides forever."*

1 Peter 1:23

Here we are at the beginning of your journey. How exciting, right? It's okay if you're nervous, but don't be afraid. You are in the hands of God. His love never fails and He NEVER leaves us. Take deep breaths. Before we get started, take a break and listen to "Let the Waters Rise" by Mike Schair. It's an amazing song that deals with fear and following God. Perfect for what you are about to go through love. Google it, let it play, read the lyrics, and let it marinate your soul.

As mentioned above, this journey of finding your identity will be like going through a spiritual birth. In the end, you will have a better understanding of who you are in the Lord. So here we are, starting something new, and taking a leap of faith. Congrats! You have now been impregnated with your destiny. Wait what (In my Despicable Me minion voice)? Yes, you read correctly. The Lord has implanted you with a new vision for your life or a burning desire to be closer to Him. You are going to have a baby! That baby, being your identity. Like any pregnancy, you need to take a test to confirm it. You may be wondering how you can take a test for a spiritual pregnancy right. The answer is simple. The Lord will test your heart. Do you remember in school at the beginning of each new school year how most teachers would have you take a pretest? They wanted to see where you were at, what you already knew, and what you didn't know. Well it's the same thing. The Lord gives us a pretest before we start anything new. He needs to know your heart is in the right place for the journey ahead. Do not let any of this information overwhelm you. Everything happens in the Lords perfect timing. Even if you don't feel ready, you probably are. Trust the Lord. Faith is the key.

## How to Take a Selfie

I remember when the Lord gave me my pretest. It was during one of the hardest times in my life, the summer of 2012. Every bad thing that happens to you is not because of the enemy or yourself? Sometimes, the Lord will allow what seems like a bad thing to happen to bring you closer to Him. Sounds super bazaar, right? Yea, the Father is something else.

That summer, I was robbed for the first time in my life. I'm from Chicago so I was aware that this was a normal thing for city life, but it had never personally affected me. The day started normally for me. At the time, I worked twelve-hour night shifts at a factory that made paper plates. It was rough coming home from work at 7 a.m. to two bright eyed young ones full of energy. I would have to do my motherly duties, which involved breakfast and playtime, then lunch until it was their naptime. During this period of my life, I was surviving on four hours of sleep per day. To make matters more difficult, I had to sleep on the couch while my kids slept in my mother's bed. After the kids and I went down for sleep, I would wake up at 4:00 p.m. to start prepping for work. Usually, the kids would have already been up for at least an hour. I used the TV to keep them still for me to finish my last hour of sleep. I would rush to the shower to get clean while they continued to watch TV. After taking a brisk shower and quickly dressing, I would pack a lunch for work. It was pretty much always the same thing. A simple sandwich, snack, and drink. Once lunch was packed, I kissed my kids and told my younger sister, Baby, I was heading out. I didn't trust daycares and my youngest child, Nani, barely spoke at all even though she was two. The company had a cafeteria where they served decent food, but as a single mother of two, I needed my money for more important matters. The route to work was fairly simple. I could get there two ways from my house. One, which consisted of two buses, and the other, which consisted of three. I usually took the route of two buses. I would have to ride the Racine bus to 69th and take the 69th bus to the street before Cicero. Afterwards, I would walk down. The problem with this route was the 69th bus was almost always late. On top of that, it was always extremely crowded. Still, I didn't want to take three buses.

A week before I was robbed, I purchased my first iPhone, the iPhone 4s. I had never cared about the iPhone, but an old friend of mine worked at Sprint and was going to hook me up with a discount. Normally, I would stick with HTCs. They were my favorite but because I was getting a discount, I figured I might as well try the iPhone out. She hooked me up and, I brought my first iPhone and a really nice case. I felt legit now. That phone was amazing. Any who, on the way to work that day I had my new phone in my pocket. I'm not sure if I was just super geeked over how much I loved what the phone could do or what, but I wasn't on my game like I should have been. As stated before, Chicago is rough, and the vultures are always swarming. I wasn't aware that the rules of the game had changed, and everyone was a target now.

As I arrived at the 69th street bus, I pulled out my phone. Honestly, if I wouldn't have pulled it out, no one would have expected me to have one. Because of my job, I looked bummy. I wore sweatpants, t-shirt, steel toe shoes, and a jacket. My hair was always pulled into a ponytail and I had my lunch bag. I could have been super rich but because of how I dressed, the hood folks paid me no mind. The phone kept ringing, alerting me of the new messages. I was talking to my good friend from high school, Vonna. I'm not even sure what we were talking about, but it must have been funny because I remember laughing extremely hard. The kind of laughter that draws attention, sadly the wrong attention.

There was this guy standing next to me waiting for the bus. I assumed he was waiting for the bus as well. For some reason, he didn't worry me. The group of guys not far from me in front of the store did but he didn't. This is why you can never judge someone by their appearances. A bus pulled up, but it was extremely crowded, and it wasn't going past Ashland. I got on but jumped right back off once I realized it wasn't going to get me anywhere. He did too. That's when my senses sharpened a bit. Something about that rubbed me the wrong way. Obviously, not enough because I pulled out that phone once again and that's when it happened. Bam! He tried to pull it out of my hand. We were fighting for my phone. I didn't want to let go, so I couldn't hit him. In retrospect, I should have kicked him with my steel toes in the groin. After hitting me in the face with his shoulder he was able to get the phone a loose. He took off running with a smile clear across his face. There were plenty of people around, but no one helped me. No one cared. There was a father and son standing at the stop but the father just watched the whole thing. He didn't even blink; maybe he thought it was a movie or something.

After the guy started running, the group of guys who worried me, came down and asked me what happened. I explained to them that I had been robbed. The father told me he thought we were playing. The group of guys thought the same thing. I gave them a look letting them know we weren't playing. The group of guys started running and looking for the guy. They looked for an hour but weren't able to find him. The father allowed me to use his phone to call the police.

They came within 30 minutes. I explained what happened, and they had me get into the car. They searched for the guy, but they were not able to find him. They even called for backup. While I was in the car, they tried to make small talk to cheer me up, but I was in shock. They offered to drop me off at work but I declined. I wasn't going to work that day. I called my job and explained the situation to my boss. He told me it was okay. That was the first time I didn't come in for work. The officers dropped me off at home and assured me they would keep looking for this guy.

## Simone Allen

I felt violated. How can you come and take something I worked so hard for away from me? I was angry. Angry with myself for not being more aware of my surroundings; I knew better. Mad at God for allowing people like that to exist. Mad at God for allowing it to happen. Why God, why? I couldn't understand why my life wasn't the way I wanted it to be. Little did I know the Lord was preparing me for something great. He was preparing my heart for His love.

I called my mom as soon as I got back home. My little sisters were confused about why I was back so early. I was angry. I began to beat the walls in the house and yell. My sister Tatiana took my kids to the second floor and distracted them. My blood was boiling. He was going to pay. I wanted to rip his throat out. I wanted him to die. Crying on the phone, I told her everything that happened. She came home immediately.

"I can track my phone. I'm going to kill him." I said to my mom when she arrived. My mom has always been tough. In a lot of ways, she raised us like boys. I had a pocketknife that she had given me a long time ago. The blade was still sharp. I had been through a lot in my life and at this stage I was bitter. I didn't really want the boy to die, but in that moment, I wanted to inflict so much pain on him to ensure that he would NEVER harm another person again.

"Calm down Simone. You need to calm down, right now." My mom stated.

"No!" I screamed at the top of my lunges while punching the wall again. "I'm going to hurt him until he can't hurt anymore. I don't care anymore. I don't care what happens to me. I'm done."

Soon the police were calling my mom to update her on the case. I had sent them a few messages of his location through the Track My Phone app. They found the boy. My mom rushed to the location but she wouldn't let me go. She made me stay and told Baby to make sure I didn't leave the house.

"Mom said you need to stay here and calm down." Baby stated. I shot her a dirty look. "Don't leave this house and do something stupid. You have kids Simone," she continued. My kids; I had forgotten about them in the heat of the moment. I do have kids. I began to calm down a bit, but I was still very angry. My mother returned soon without my phone or any hope of it being found. He was long gone with my phone. I honestly believed the police found him, but they didn't understand how to use an iPhone so wasn't able to investigate properly. They were still using flip phones. The next day I called Sprint and explained the situation. I had to open up another line to get the phone at the decent price but I decided on a different phone. Two days later, I returned to work with a bandage on my face and went about my business. My sister, Baby, or my mom took me to work for about two months before I was comfortable to ride the bus again. I never took that route to work again, and I never took my phone out at the bus stop or while I rode the bus. When people came too close, I would get suspicious and start paying more attention. To this day, I am a bit jumpier but definitely more aware of my surroundings at all time even though I no longer live in Chicago.

Exercise time. Today I humbly thank God for protecting me during that robbery. Not just from the guy causing damage, but also from me doing even more harm to my life, his life, and my kids' life. At the time, I didn't have a relationship with God, so I had no spiritual covering. I didn't pray, but because of His grace, he protected me and covered me regardless. It is frightening to think how much I let the enemy influence me that that summer. To think, I almost allowed him to push me to serious violations over a phone. A phone that gets updated every year at that! Nobody is greater than God! You may think that God is ignoring you during your storm, but I promise you, he's not. He has covered and protected you even though you can't see it yet. Can you remember a time when the Lord saved you from making a big mistake? Write it down and give the Lord praise for saving you. It's by His grace that we are here today. A great song to listen to during this time is "Nobody Greater" by Vashawn Mitchell. Google it, let it play, read the lyrics, and let it marinate your soul.

Being robbed was just the beginning of the test. I would be tested a lot more during that summer. However, the end of it came when a guy rejected me. Yep, that's right, a guy. During that summer, there was this guy I was dating, or so I thought (he later clarified that this was not the case, in a text no less). We were doing everything two people in a relationship would do, actually what married couples do. Yep, you guessed it, premarital sex. I knew when this guy approached me and we started getting to know each other that he was broken. I figured this out the first time we hung out. He came over one day to watch movies and drink. We watched about two movies and drank Patron. Things were going well. I told him about my life and he shared his. He seemed different from the typical guy I would normally date. Most of which were absolutely the worst for me. As the evening was coming close to an end and after having way too many sips of Patron, I told him what I thought about him. I told him I thought he was broken. That statement made him upset, and he was ready to go shortly after. While waiting at the bus stop, he told me all sorts of great things about how much he liked me. In my heart, I knew none of it could be true because of his brokenness. I still allowed him to pursue me because I thought I could fix him. I thought my love was the key to his happiness even if it meant sacrificing my own happiness. He wasn't what I needed.

After a while of us doing things we should not have been doing, he became distant. Me being me, I decided to ask him about it. In case you're wondering what that means, it means I can be blunt at times, especially if I'm hurt. Not just blunt but very petty at that. Mix this with that fact that I tend to over analyze things and have a pretty dangerous concoction. Honestly, my mind won't let go of something until I know the facts. I should have become a detective. Anyway, after approaching him I found out he went back to the very woman who had broken his heart. Hurt and upset from feeling used, I sent him the longest text in history explaining why he completely sucked. I was more than upset; I was seething with vengeful anger. It made no sense to me why he would go back to that woman after everything he had said about her. On top of that, all of this was happening about two weeks after I was robbed! It's true what they say: hurt people, hurt people. He was hurt so he hurt me; I was hurt so I hurt him, with my words. The woman he went back to had to be hurt as well to make him feel that way. It's a constant cycle that few of us are aware of. None of us knew our worth or the true love of the Lord. Had we truly known what real love was, we wouldn't have been chasing the worldly kind. When you accept God's love for you, then you start to learn how valuable you are. You are precious; stop giving yourself away to people who don't deserve you.

Here I was, yet again, dealing with the same feelings I had with the robbery. Anger followed by rejection, hurt, and confusion. How could God continue to let things happen to me? What was so wrong with me that I continued to go through this repeated cycle with love? Continuing the cycle of the hurt, made me bitter inside. The enemy whispered lies into my ear that made me feel as if I had every right to hurt that man for what he did. The truth is, I had no right at all. That wasn't my lane. I should have never turned my tongue into a weapon and attacked him to his core. Those were words that I would need to repent for later.

With all of these emotions, I needed to deal with them alone so I went to the beach in the middle of the night around 11 p.m. I Sat there watching the waves, and I began to weep. I wept tears that were filled with anger, hurt, disappointment, rejection, confusion etc. I looked at the sky and I asked the Lord, "God, why? Why me? I can't take this anymore, I'm falling apart. I need your help. If you don't help me, I don't think I'm going to make it. I'm going to die." This was going to be the end for me. I had taken as much as I thought I could handle in life. I hated the thoughts that ran through my mind of suicide. The lies the enemy whispered in my ear and I sadly believed. What about my children? It made me feel guilty,

## How to Take a Selfie

and I pegged myself as the worst mother in the world... but God!

Sitting at the beach was the first time I heard the Lord's voice clearly. With tears on my face and my feelings out there, I looked down at a mouse and then looked to the sky. That's when I heard Him say, "fly" while watching a plane go by. I knew where I needed to go. I knew at that point if I was going to stay in Chicago, I was going to die spiritually and maybe even physically.

Exercise time. Reading that probably brought your spirit down a bit. Your emotions are probably going through the motions while you are relating. Take a break and take a SELFIE!! Yep, as you are, don't try to cheat. Remember, we're being transparent here. Take the selfie while listening to "Beautiful Things" by Gungor. Indeed, a very beautiful song. Google it, let it play, read the lyrics, and let it marinate your soul.

As you can see, at that very moment I was completely broken. Nothing left to give of myself. I needed my Father like never before, and it was time I allowed Him to enter my life. God can take your dust and make something beautiful. That's what this journey is about. You may feel broken, lost, and confused now, but that's exactly what He wants to take from you. If it weren't for all the bad things I went through that summer, much more to be reveled later, I wouldn't have come to Him at that time. He allowed me to be broken so that He could repair me, the correct way. There was no true foundation. In truth, I was broken long before any of those things happened. He knew what it would take for me to finally surrender to Him for healing. He wanted to create a true foundation for me in Him. A foundation that could never be broken no matter what storm came. God will allow you to go through everything the enemy throws at you because He knows in the end you will come to Him. Understand that God sees your ending at the beginning. He knows everything about you, including how many hairs you have on your head.

Are you ready to take your pretest? Is your heart ready to surrender to the Lord? Here is a scripture for beginning your journey and trusting the Lord's plan for your life. My absolute favorite, Jeremiah 29:11. Study these scriptures and ask the Holy Spirit to guide you to more. Write down those scriptures here. Once your heart is ready it's time to call the doctor.

## How to Take a Selfie

Dance time. Listen to "Multiplied," by Needtobreathe. This song says everything about surrendering to the Lord in a positive and radiant way. It is sure to move you in more ways than one and bring joy to your life. Get silly, let loose, and have fun. Enjoy loves!

> If God is your partner, make your plans BIG!
> –D.L. Moody

## Chapter 2

# Call the Doc; Lay Your Heart Upon the Lord

*"There were times when I knew I was in a terrible situation, but I also knew that it wouldn't last forever. Those are the moments when you have to remind yourself that this experience is a defining moment in your life, but you are not defined by it."*

-Ronda Rousey

Remember in the prolog I told you about a song called "Lay it Down by Sanctus Real?" Well, if you haven't followed directions and listened to it, I suggest you do it now. It will give you a clear understanding of this chapter.

After you take a test, you need to call the doctor and start seeking prenatal care, correct? Well, God our Father is the ultimate doctor; he has ALL the answers and medicine needed for you to be healed. Jesus is a healer! To be healed, you need to acknowledge your issues. For example, right before I started to build my relationship with God, I dealt with the enemy's voice often. I was depressed but hid it well. The world had no idea but I was dying inside, loves.

Remember in chapter one I said there was more to tell on that life changing summer? Well the summer of 2012, right before I moved to Virginia, was the worst for me mentally. I cried every day for 30 days straight. When I say every day, I mean every day. It never failed, after I came home from work, put my kids to bed and all were sleep, I wept. I felt like nothing. The enemy had convinced me that my life would never amount to what I wanted, I was a horrible parent because I was a single parent, and I would never be loved. For some reason when you're in pain, the mind tends to bring up older memories that caused you pain too. This only happens of course if you haven't been healed of those situations. Obviously, I had not. Horrid memories of my past surfaced everyday causing more pain and leaving me tormented. The most hurtful one being the domestic abuse I endured from my youngest child's father. It was something that I didn't want to remember and didn't want to talk about. Despite my best effort to act like that part of my life didn't happen, the truth crept up.

One day during that summer as I lay on the couch trying to sleep at night during one of my days off, the ugly memories started to bother me. It had been at least a year or so since the last time I had been abused by my child's father, yet the wounds were still fresh. I continued to toss and turn trying to push the memory into the back of my head. Nothing was working. He had laid his hands on me on three different occasions. The worst time, being the last. This was the one that bothered me the most. The memory wouldn't fade away.

That day started like any other normal day. I tended to my daughter in our bedroom, the one room we once shared. He was the first and only guy I had moved in with, something that I clearly shouldn't have done. My son was at my mom's house spending time with my family. The room the kids and I occupied had the TV in it. He had moved his stuff into the room across the hall. After drinking, he decided he would come in and take the TV to watch football. I contested. Our daughter was watching TV and they were in the middle of a movie. My saying no sent him into a rage. He tried to push us out, but I wouldn't budge. This only made things worse for us. Determined and drunk, he made a horrible decision. He decided that he would get us out no matter what it took. He stormed out of the room pass me. I assumed I had won the battle and went back to attending to my daughter. Shortly after, I noticed smoke and a foul odor creep into the room. He had thrown a roach bomb into our room. I grabbed my daughter and ran out of the room. She was still under one at the time. She started crying horribly as I began to cough. Neither of us could breathe, we desperately needed fresh air. I took her to the back porch for some fresh air. She stopped crying eventually. Livid, I knew he would need to pay for that. I would make him pay for this. Was a football game that important that you would harm your own child? I couldn't believe what had happen. I thought about all the ways I could make him suffer. With the enemy heavily in my ear, after several hours of thinking of how to make him suffer, I decided I would spike his drink with a laxative. I imagined how cruel and embarrassing it would be if he would crap his pants while hanging with his friends. The problem was I didn't have any to put into his drink. That didn't stop me from thinking about how to damage his ego.

## How to Take a Selfie

He had long left since throwing the bomb. I called my cousin and expressed how I felt. I was tired of him, and I was ready to move on. I told her what happened and how I wanted to react. We laughed at how funny it *would* have been. None of this was Godly, not one bit. After getting off the phone with her, I felt a lot better. My daughter and I continued about our day without any care.

Night came and so did he. The door slammed open to the room. To this very day, I'm not sure if he pushed it really hard or kicked it. Nevertheless, the effect was still the same. Yelling, he told me how he was going to kill me. Over and over he stated the following "You stupid b**** you put something in my drink. I'm going to kill you. I'm going to f****** kill you." He began to choke me. He threw me around like I was nothing. He bit me, leaving the biggest bruise on my chest. He beat me endlessly. Somehow, I was able to reach for the phone and I called his mother for help. That's the last thing I remember about that night.

I tried to make sense of what was happening. I never actually put something in his drink. He wasn't even there when I said I would try it. It didn't take me long to figure out that one of his cousins told him about my conversation. She refused to tell the whole story because she would've had to admit it never officially happened. Several of his cousins and grandmother stayed in the house we occupied. It was owned by his mother. At the time when I moved in there, he was the only one living in the house. Those same cousins and grandmother were downstairs while this whole thing happened. No one came to help me though, and no one cared. When he stopped hitting me, I fled to the bathroom and dialed 911. I wasn't sure if he was done or needed a quick breath, but I ran. I could hear my daughter crying her eyes out. She was scared and unable to understand what was happening. The 911 operator stayed on the phone with me until I heard the door slam and he left. While I was on the phone and before he left, I heard one of his cousins nonchalantly tell him "grandma said leave that girl alone,." as if we were five and he was simply being a pest. Not as if he was physically abusing me. Not as if they had heard death threats being made or if they hadn't heard my scream stop or call for help. Nope just a simple "leave that girl alone" was the only help I was given.

The police arrived on the scene rather quickly, and he was out front calm and cool as if nothing had happened. Something about his cool demeanor made the police think he was innocent. As customary, they began to ask what happened. He told them nothing had happened, and I told them the truth. They didn't believe me though. They stated that this was typical baby mama drama, and I was probably just mad at him. Mad? I was furious. Although my entire body ached I could only think to show them the scar on my neck. They looked unimpressed. Surprisingly, they were female officers. They pulled our records. His was clean, but I had been arrested when I was 19 for getting into a fist fight with a girl. Like idiots, we both pressed charges on each, other which the court dropped. It was the only time I've been in trouble with the law. It didn't matter to them. They believed him and not me.

They put him the squad car and arrested him because they had no choice. I was pressing charges. I informed the officers his family was there during the abuse and that his mom was on the phone when it happened. His family lied. I don't know if they ever questioned his mom though. This was the third time he had put his hands on me, and she knew about the prior abuse. The female officer handed me the police report, which was supposed to contain the court date. I would find out later that the court date was falsified. She believed him so much that she purposely gave me the wrong court date so that I would miss it which would have the charges dropped. With uneasiness, I went back into the house avoiding the disgusting stares from his family. I could hear the nasty talk about me and how one of them had been hit in the mouth by a bat by her child's father, and she didn't call the police. To them I was in the wrong because I didn't take the abuse. To this day, they continue to coddle him and hate me. The Lord has helped me to forgive them all, but it has been a long journey. With no time to waste I began to pack my stuff, and I called my family for help. My mom and sisters showed up. I forgot a pair of shoes, the pair that he brought me for my birthday. When I went back to get them, they were gone. I never saw them again, and it's probably a good thing. I probably wouldn't have worn them again anyway. That would be the last time he actually put his hands on me though he tried one very last time. However, that time I wouldn't stand for it and he put us out.

The memory wouldn't fade and it was bothering me more and more. Everything I had been dealing with in my life was bothering me. This ugly cocktail of lies, truth, and memories ate away at me until there was almost nothing left. Constantly I had a feeling that there was an intense battle for my life between God and Satan. It looked bleak, but this is why you should learn to walk by faith and not by sight. God was fighting for me. He knew my worth, and He wouldn't stop until I was His again.

Our Lord is faithful, loving, and merciful! At times, we believe God has forgotten us, we let the enemy deceive us, but it's all a lie. You are worth love, you are loved, and God loves you. As you can see I needed healing, but I didn't fully know that God could heal me and take away the pain I harbored. It would take me being pushed to the edge before I would allow Him to operate on me. Do you know that despite everything you have been through, God can heal you? Do you really believe it? Well He can and He will. All you have to do is ask! Of course, it took that last straw with the guy before I gave all in, but He used all of it to lead me to Him anyway. He knew that if He continued to pursue me, eventually I would get tired of running.

Exercise time. Take a moment to think about some areas in your life that you feel are too ugly for anyone to see. Go look deep within yourself, and pull out what is causing you pain. Write it down a separate piece of paper, and give it to God. Nothing is too ugly for Him and nothing can be hidden. I know love, it's painful to reach into the darkness, but it's only painful until it's healed. While you are completing this exercise, listen to "Unstoppable Love" by Jesus Culture featuring Kim Walker Smith. This song states how much God pursues us and reminds us how he yearns for us to be His. After you are done, listen to "Spirit Break Out" by Kim Walker Smith. As you listen to the music, make sure you allow yourself to be unguarded. Allow God to break your walls down. Allow the Holy Spirit to invade woo you like never before. Seriously God is the ultimate romantic! Enjoy your moments with Him. Remember, Google it, let it play, read the lyrics, and let it marinate your soul.

Shortly after I moved to VA and started attending my current church, Cornerstone International Worship Center, the Lord began to work on my depression and mental battles. Again, that same day the Lord called me to the altar. While weeping and praying as hard as I could a prophet touched my forehead and told me to stop letting the enemy trick me into believing that I am crazy because I'm not. I knew this was from the Lord because I had been praying and weeping for deliverance. I wanted to be free from this constant battle; Free of the pain from the memories, of the feeling of abandonment. I wanted to be free from it *all* all. During those 30 days of depression, I knew there was a battle for my life. The Holy Spirit made it clear that God and the enemy wanted my mind, and if I didn't start to truly let the Lord in, I would die. Of course, I didn't know at the time it was the Holy Spirit guiding me, but I knew exactly what was going on.

Again, It is time to start laying your heart before the Lord. Write down your struggles. Be as transparent as possible. He already knows but you need to acknowledge them yourself (John 4:23-24). This is the time to get real. I mean no makeup, no filter, hair tied, no bra and sweat pants on real. For you guys that may be reading this, get boxers and socks real. All jokes aside you have to let go of superficial things and come truly as you are in this moment. You probably feel like you have already done this but to be honest, this is one exercise that will constantly be repeated in your life. The truth is, we often believe we are healed in an area until something reminds us that we aren't. Despite what you stated earlier, you need to dig a bit deeper. You need to go further. It's all going to hurt but, again, it only hurts until it's healed.

Start researching scripture that matches your problem. For example, I struggled with not feeling loved. A great scripture for this is John 3:16: "For the Lord so loved the world he gave his only begotten son." Stand on His word for it is the truth. What scriptures help you with your struggles? Write them down. I don't know about you, but I struggle with learning scripture. John 3:16 was the first scripture I memorized. I use this scripture as a reminder of how great His love is. It also helps that this scripture is on the bottom of every Forever 21 bag. What? I know right! Don't believe me next time you go shopping check it out for yourself.

Exercise time. Guess what? Yep, you guessed it; it's time to take a selfie!! You're probably not in the mood, right? Spirit man feeling a little weak, tear stains on your cheek? Great, this is the PERFECT time to take a selfie. Remember this entire book is about spiritual healing and finding your identity. You must be as transparent as possible. That means taking pictures at times when you feel a picture isn't warranted. Take that "ugly" beautiful picture. It's time to start seeing ourselves the way God

## How to Take a Selfie

sees us. We are beautiful. He only makes beautiful creations. So you can relax and stop comparing yourself to the world's standards because you aren't of the world love.

Take advantage of your resources. If you feel like you cannot lay your heart upon the Lord, ask a spiritual leader to help you pray and to pray for you. Sometimes it is hard to face the truth by ourselves. Your spiritual leader can help you with this and teach you how to do it on your own. You don't need all the pieces of the puzzle to start. Start with one piece and add another and another. Eventually, the puzzle will be whole. If you haven't been able to identify your problems or scriptures to help with this, now is the time to go to your spiritual leader. Do that before you continue. Aye, no peeking; let's be obedient. We lay our hearts upon the Lord because no one else can heal them There is no one else. We often think we can fix our problems all on our own but we can't. Not even a little. When you are pregnant and you visit the doctor, you tell them all your symptoms, right? You don't hold anything back because if you do, it may harm your baby. You want the doctors to run the entire test and give you the answers, right? That is a normal part of life for many of us. In fact, you probably suffer a bit from hypochondria. See a new mole and think it's the end for you? Yep, I do that sometimes too. You're not alone. Let's join HA together. No but in all seriousness, we bombard the doctors with questions and demand answers yet we hide our symptoms from God, "Side eye" as if he can't see them already. Ever play hide and seek with a young child? They hide in the most obvious places, right? You take your time to find them even though you clearly see them. We do this because we know if we find them right away, it spoils the game. The same happens with our Father. He knows your problems before you do and already has the solutions. However, His timing is perfect. He knows just when to find you. You feel hidden but you're not. You couldn't hide no matter how hard you tried; he will always be able to see past our best hiding place.

Let's dance. A great upbeat song that talks about giving your heart to Jesus is "Live with Abandon" by the News Boys. "I want to live with abandon, give you all that I am, every part of my heart Jesus, I place in your hand." Best line from the song to me. It speaks to my soul on every level. It fits perfectly with our emotions right now.

## How to Take a Selfie

We are laying it all out there! Listen to the song guys. Remember to Google it, let it play, read the lyrics, and let it marinate your soul.

How do you feel now? Has there been a shift? When we lay our hearts before the Lord, a burden is lifted. Even while still standing in the storm, you're calmed. How can you be calm in the middle of a storm? Our God is great! We give Him our problems, and He gives us peace. No one but our God can do this. After I began to truly give me problems to the Lord, I was gifted with a joy and peace that I had never experienced prior. It felt like taking a really great bath with bubbles, candles and music. When I emerged, I felt cleansed. Nothing was perfect, and my life was still a mess but things were changing, and that particular storm was beginning to clear. After every storm there is a rainbow, Jesus is clothed in a rainbow! God has a sense of humor, doesn't he?

Simone Allen

Chapter 3

# Change Your Lifestyle

*"The God of your moment, of your small moments is the God of your life."*

-Mia Deneen Smith

Exercise time. "But first let me take a selfie." Grab that phone, selfie stick, and get to it. I want you to see your face right now. Tell yourself how beautiful or handsome you are. Remember, you are a total BOSS. XOXOXO

At this point, it's time for you to start making healthy changes to your lifestyle. I'm not telling you to go on an all kale diet or anything of that nature but it's time to make better choices. On your road to identity you start to notice that things are not the same. Your old lifestyle begins to feel outdated and foreign. That's because what once was, no longer fits. The closer your relationship with God grows, the more you want to be Christ like. This means doing things differently than you did before.

After my move to Virginia, I started praying to the Lord heavily. I had this urge to speak with Him daily. Like, all the time! Praise and worship became a daily part of my routine. It wasn't because I was forced to do so. It's because it felt good to do so. I never knew that it would feel so good and never understood it before. The old nasty habits I had were slowly going away, and I was being transformed into something better. As time passed, I found myself making decisions based on being Christ like. I no longer wanted to be worldly.

If all of this confuses you a bit, that's okay. I'll clarify. After you find out you're having a baby, you go to the doctor to express your concerns, and you begin to make better choices because you're carrying a child. You can't drink anymore or smoke. You start being picky about what you put into your body, on your skin, etc. You don't go out as much because you need rest. You make choices that will help you have a healthy child. Some of you are probably having difficulty relating because you have never had a child or you're a guy. However, this rule applies to everything. If you want something, you make better

## How to Take a Selfie

choices to get it. Want to join the Varsity team? You train, exercise, eat better, and focus more. Want to go to college? You study, hang out less, etc. When you want something, you make the necessary changes and sacrifices to get it. Finding your identity is very similar. You have to make the necessary changes and sacrifices to find it.

Exercise time! What are some of your spiritual goals when it comes to finding your identity? Write them down below. Have you started to make healthy changes in your life? Write down some of the changes you have noticed thus far here. Here are a few scriptures related to new beginnings and positive changes. "I am a new creature." (2 Corinthians 5:17 NIV). "I am forgiven all my sins are washed in the blood." (Ephesians 1:7 NIV). "I am being changed into His image." (Philippians 1:6 NIV). It's important to surround yourself with company who are succeeding in the areas you wish to grow. For example, if you want to eat better, you surround yourself with people who meal prep, work out, etc. The same goes spiritually. You cannot continue to be around people, in environments that can stunt your growth.

The change is going to happen without you noticing it at times. While I noticed that I spoke to the Lord more,

I didn't notice the little changes I made. Other people noticed them in me first. People will notice your change quickly, especially the people you were close to before you started to build your relationship with God. I had stopped using profanity for the most part. I still used it (which is wrong) but very seldom. My upbringing was in a family who heavily used profanity. It was a very intricate part of my life. I remember my granddad would say hello with profanity. Seriously, he insulted you, praised you, and nurtured you with profanity. It flowed out his mouth like it truly belonged. It was like that for everyone in my family, including myself. I needed to make a change and the closer I became with God, the less I used profanity. When I stopped using it for the most part, I picked up how much they used it. It was as if I could hear for the very first time, and I did not like it. Seriously, it disgusted me to hear it and say it. It's like when you are interested in buying a certain type of car. Soon you began to notice that vehicle every time you see it on the street. Profanity became very much like that. I remember counting how many times someone used profane language during our conversations. Often times, I couldn't fully listen to what was being said because the profanity distracted me. The

## How to Take a Selfie

Lord was evolving me and that would include even the smallest details such as my language.

During this transition from old to new, I started sharing the gospel with others. This was completely unexpected because I couldn't quote scriptures, but I had learned a lot from spending time with the Lord. (I still can't quote a ton of scriptures lol). Majority of the time, I didn't realize I was sharing the gospel. I thought I was simply sharing my testimony. I wanted everyone around me to feel the love, peace, and joy I felt from God. It was amazing, and no words could express how I felt. It was like nothing made sense, but everything made sense. BAZAR, I know! My praise and worship became so intense I no longer cared who was around. Chains were being released, and I felt like I could fly. I wasn't bound to my old habits anymore. The Lord had set me free. I'm sure you guys have seen the movie *Rio* by Dream Work Studios, right? Remember when Jewel finally got those chains off? How high she soared? That's how I felt, like finally, for the first time, I was free. Free to be who I was all along. It's as if I needed permission to be her. Maybe it's because, since I could remember, Satan made me believe that everything about me was wrong. From my looks, my naturally creative gifts, to being nerdy and weird, and I believed his lies. But when someone told me about the power and love of the Lord! When I accepted it truly in my heart! That burning, the comfort, and the joy were like everything I had been searching for. I was unmistakably his creation. The same applies to you Love. "I am God's workmanship, created in Christ Jesus for good works." (Ephesians 2:10 NIV).

People will notice the changes in you before you do. My family quickly pointed out how much I had changed. I got labeled a Bible thumper. To be honest, the more I blindly followed the Lord the more I was branded as crazy. Seriously, my mom thought I went mad for a season or too. In her defense, I did go "crazy." Crazy about the Lord, anyway! Just to clarify, I am NOT a bible thumper; I'm still learning scriptures people. (FYI Bible thumpers are usually people that know that bible from cover to cover.) They felt like I had been converted into a cult or something. Like I had drunk the juice or been exposed to my older sister far too long. To them, she had poisoned me with her nonsense and I was becoming a mini version of her with all of my Jesus talk. The truth is I wasn't being like her, but I was becoming like the Christ in her. The Christ who lives within each and every one of us. It was hard for them to tell the difference because they still had worldly eyes. To the outsiders, it appeared as if I had gone bat crazy, but for fellow spiritually mature Christians it was a completely different story. It was hard for me. As many positive changes the Lord was making through me, there were still a lot that needed to be rebuilt. The spirit of rejection still lingered in me. It would until I got delivered and accepted sonship. We'll discuss more on this in the next chapter.

I lost people as I continued to change. Seriously, it's not like I had a lot to start with in the beginning but, just about all the ones I had were removed. The things that appealed to me before didn't carry the same thrill anymore. My friends thought I had become lame. They thought I was completely tripping. Those friendships had to end. I still love each and every one of them, but our lives drifted into different spaces. Not everyone is going to accept you making healthy life changes. Mostly because they don't understand it yet and that's okay, love. They aren't able to comprehend it yet. Not only that but you'll learn that some friendships are only supposed to last for a season, not a lifetime. That doesn't make the person a bad person, but they aren't equipped to move into your next season with you. In life, you will also be this seasonal person to others. Sometimes it doesn't work because they didn't belong in your life at all. You let in a complete imposter because of your lack of discernment. I've done this so many times, so know that you are not alone. However, because of this, I had my door privileges revoked by the Lord. Confused? Allow me to explain, love. As a child, we are not allowed to open the door for strangers, right? When we hear a knock or the doorbell, we go and get our parent. As we got older our door privileges were more lenient. Well, when you start this journey, you are a babe in Christ. You thought you were grown because of age but you are indeed the opposite spiritually. Before Christ, you let complete strangers into your life because you didn't use your discernment. On your journey He will do a clean sweep and start removing those buglers who do nothing but steal from you. Nope they steal things that are far more precious and valuable than your material possessions. Some of those inner jewels consist of peace, love, happiness, and time. You let in strangers and now they have to go. Your door privileges will be revoked until you have matured and learned. God is now in control of who is allowed. You may say "it's not that serious Simone," or you may believe a certain person is safe. Please don't be so naïve. It's very serious who is in your life. You are the sum of the company you keep. The Lord is the best Father there is. Trust me when I say He doesn't play about His child. Also, don't assume anyone is safe. It doesn't matter what their title or position is in your life. If God says they do not belong, trust and believe they will be removed. You can do it His way or the hard way. In the end, the result will still be same. Except His way is a lot less painful. I've tried to hold on to so many, and He allowed them to use and abuse me until I was obedient. Similar to if you let a burglar into your house and allow them to stay. Don't be surprised when they take you for everything you got. You saw the warnings on the news and you chose to ignore it. Please don't make these simple mistakes. If the Lord says let them go, do both of you a favor, and release them.

You are going to have to be strong for yourself. The enemy will try to use familiarity as a reason to pull you back, to stop you from continuing on this journey. Don't worry because you are not in this alone. God is with you every step of the way. There are people who are praying for your journey who you don't even know. He has you covered. It is your time and you can do this. You are a champ, an overcomer, you are great, and you are loved. I love you and He loves you. You have an army of people on your side; Heaven is on your side; the angels are on your side; Jesus is on your side. You can do this! No matter what you get hit with, know that this is only temporary.

Exercise time. Write down some of the changes others have noticed in you. Compare this list to the one you wrote earlier. How are they similar? How do are they different? Make a list of everyone you felt you have lost. Pray for them. Remember God loves us all. They may not have a relationship with Him now, but that doesn't mean they won't ever have one. You may be the missing key to them giving their life to the Lord. Be sure to set an example because believe it or not, they are watching to see just who He is in you.

Dance time! You are probably feeling emotional and overwhelmed. You may even feel alone, but you're not. Listen to "Closer Than You Know" by Hillsong United. This beautiful song explains how Heaven is closer than you know. God is closer than you know. I pray that it gives you strength to continue on your journey. I pray He ministers to your heart, and you feel his love on another level. Don't run as the song says, "Don't turn away from me, for my love won't be undone. Don't hide your face from me, for my light has surely come." Next listen and dance to "He Turned It" by Tye Tribbett. Get up and worship. Think about the fact that Satan thought he had you. But God! Google it, let it play, read the lyrics, and let it marinate your soul. We love you!

Simone Allen

# YOU'RE SUCH A

[Insert Photo Here]

# TOTAL ROCK STAR

Chapter 4

# Finding the Sex: Son-ship, Letting Go of the Orphan Spirit

*"You cannot help the body of Christ if you do not know what part of the body you are. An ear can only be an ear."*

–Simone Star

For many finding out the sex of a baby is the biggest part of a pregnancy. It's one of the greatest joys. Will it be a son or a daughter? Or perhaps both, and son and a daughter! I remember when I was pregnant with my firstborn, my son Jeremiah. I was relieved to know my firstborn would be a son. It gave me great joy because I felt I could not mother a daughter. When my next born turned out to be my daughter Nyimah, I was overwhelmed. Honestly, the moment the ultrasound tech told me she was a girl my joy dropped. My blood began to boil. "A girl," I thought. No, not a girl. I was so hurt and angry that I didn't wait for the tech to wipe the gel off my belly before I quickly leaped up and stormed out the room. I could hear the lady ask if I was okay as I stormed out, but I ignored her. A girl. This was too much. How could I be a proper mother to my daughter when I had seen few great mother daughter relationships? I wasn't this smitten girly girl. I had been a tomboy for most of my life, and I rarely got along with girls. How was I going to be close with her? My relationship with my mother had been ugly for most of my childhood and adult life. I felt greatly unliked when it came to her. I knew she loved me but I felt she didn't like me. I felt like a burden to her. We were too much alike, and it caused us to constantly crash. It pained me to know that I would have a daughter because in my mind, I would fail her. I feared that she would go through similar emotions I had with my mother. You see, in retrospect, I had been dealing with the orphan spirit for most of my life. Growing up, there was no father for me. The only male figure in my life was my granddad that I was extremely close to because I felt he was the only member of my family who attempted to accept me. A little girl with no father and a mother as distant yet close as the moon was not to mother a girl. It felt like an unaccomplishable goal. I felt that there was no way I was going to be able to do this. However, my feelings didn't matter at that point. She was coming regardless, and it was time I started to get myself together for her.

During my pregnancy with my daughter, I began to promise my daughter that I would do better for her. I would be close and tell her every day that she was loved. If she were to be a girly girl, which she most definitely is, I would join her in activities that I wouldn't normally do. My goal was to establish a healthy relationship with my daughter, which in fact we have thanks to God. She is indeed my shadow and we are indeed close. Words of affirmation would not be enough. I would have to put in the work. In order to have a healthy relationship with my kids, I needed to get rid of my orphan spirit.

What exactly is the orphan spirit? "The orphan spirit causes one to live life as if he does not have a safe and secure place in the Father's heart. He feels he has no place of affirmation, protection, comfort, belonging, or affection. Self-oriented, lonely, and inwardly isolated, he has no one from whom to draw Godly inheritance.

Therefore, he has to strive, achieve, compete, and earn everything he gets in life. It easily leads to a life of anxiety, fears, and frustration." (Jack Frost)

Another way to identify the orphan spirit is through common characteristics. Here is a chart from the article From Slavery to Sonship (2) by Jack and Trista Frost of Shilon Place Ministries (PO Box 5, Conway, SC 29528) that helps you see the differences between the hearts of an orphan versus the heart of son-ship.

Exercise time! After reading what the orphan spirit is, there probably are a lot of thoughts running through your mind. Do you identify with the orphan spirit? I had a mom but no father and I was still an orphan because I did not identify God as my true Father. Had I known this already. I would have the orphan spirit regardless of the status of my parents. Take the time now to self -reflect, and write down your feelings in a letter to your Father. Tell God of all the ways you felt abandoned and alone. Tell him the ways you identify with the orphan spirit. Pour your heart out, love. It's okay. Sometimes we feel the need to hide our feelings from God. We think we may be punished if we tell Him how we really feel. That right there is a key point of suffering from the orphan spirit.

Someone with the heart of son-ship knows that there is nothing you can say or do that will stop God from loving you. Here are some scriptures on son-ship Romans 8:15, John 14:18 and John 3:16. Other great teachings on the orphan spirit include teachings by Dr. Faith W. and Jack Frost's book Experiencing Fathers Embrace. I encourage you to explore son-ship in great debt. To truly understand that you are a child of God, to accept his love, and obtain the heart of son-ship is going to be one of the best things to ever happen to you. You will experience freedom as the burden of the orphan spirit is lifted. Pause and think about that freedom for a minute. Just sit and really meditate. Can you feel the chains breaking off? Does it make your heart smile? It should!

When the Lord wants to do something in your life, He does it with or without your permission. I didn't realize I had been carrying the orphan spirit, and it wasn't until he began to pull it out of me that I realized it was deeply rooted in me. It took lots of studying the word, praying, and establishing a strong relationship. There were times when I didn't understand that fragments of the spirit still remained but the Lord is faithful and patient. He continued to operate on my heart even when

## Simone Allen

I didn't think I would make it. There were many layers to the orphan spirit, one of the biggest being forgiveness. I had to go to the root of the spirit, the cause of it. I had to forgive those who I felt hurt me, including God. I had to understand that nothing is out of God's control, and He knows the true plan for each of our lives.

You see, as an orphan I felt I had to earn God's love. For His love, I had to constantly come home with good grades, always do the right things, etc. There was little room for error because I felt if I were to mess up He wouldn't love me. Boy, was I wrong. God worked on my mindset first. He got rid of these thoughts. He loves us, PERIOD. No if, ands, or buts. You do not have to work to earn His love because it is already given. I couldn't believe this and doubted it greatly at first. He is such a great Father; He always gives you perspective so that you truly grasp the concept. He gave me an example of my children. There is NOTHING my children could ever do to make me stop loving them. I will always love them. Well, surely the Lord is a better parent; so imagine your love for someone multiplied by infinity. That is the power of His love. It is greater than the sun, stars, and moon. It is infinite!

How to Take a Selfie

Every example on the side of the heart of an orphan reflected me before God operated and blessed me with a new heart and mindset. The more he healed me, the more my heart became that of a true daughter of Christ. That pressure lifted, gave me joy. However, we never go through trials and tribulations for ourselves. We go through them to be an example for others. It was important for me to understand this so that I could share this knowledge with my children and others. My family has had the generational curse of being worldly fatherless. Meaning just about all of us grew up in a single parent house hold with a strong mother and no father. In fact men are in such a short supply in my family that you could consider them an endangered species. This has also affected my children. Because of God's love for me, I have been able to break this curse and to teach my children that God is their ultimate Father. They understand that they are not orphans but children of the kingdom. They feel His love and accept it. They understand that they are not bound to performance for a master. Truly, this is all because of His love. Once you understand something, you have that knowledge forever. My children will forever know that they are loved by the King of Kings, the greatest parent, God.

## Simone Allen

Exercise time! I know you just did an exercise, but you had a very different emotion when you began the previous exercise. Towards the end, you began to feel better as you imagined and prayed the chains away. I want you to take a selfie with the thought of freedom. How does your new sense of freedom feel? I say you get up and shake your body because you're free baby! Do a little dance, laugh a little, and have some fun. My playlist suggestion is "Life in Color" by One Republic and "Run Wild" by For King and Country as a great way to inform you that you are no longer a slave. I totally heart you right now because you are such a rock star!

How to Take a Selfie

Chapter 5

# Your Name

Congratulations on making it to this point of the book. This journey has probably been one of the most difficult things you have ever had to do in your life, but you are putting in the work. Clap emoji to you loves. Do you know the meaning of your name? Your name believe it or not is one of the key points to your identity. Even if you do not love or like your name, it still has a meaning behind it. When my mother was giving birth to me, she wanted me to have a name similar to her name Leashia. I'm not entirely sure if she initially wanted to name me Leashia Jr. or not. She had this tendency of naming her kids in various ways after her. Now, before you make the side eye face, my mother is a Sr. and the sister right under me is Jr. They are both female and they aren't the only mother daughter duo using Sr./Jr. It's more common than you think. Don't believe me, Google it. Now somewhere in the naming process, my grandmother decided to name me Simone. She named me after her favorite soap opera actress. I am the only grandchild she has named. The Holy Spirit prompted my grandmother to name me at the point of delivery.

Growing up I never thought much of the meaning of my name. I loved it but people always mispronounced it. Although, it is a fairly easy name. Nevertheless, I loved my name despite not knowing the meaning of it. It wasn't until the beginning of April 2015 that the Lord had me search for the meaning of my name. My name means "one who hears." It is the female version of the Hebrew name Simon. If you are familiar with the Bible, then you know who Simon Peter is. God gave Simon the name Peter later in his life. Peter means "a rock" and again Simon means one who hears. Simon Peter was a man with a solid foundation who heard the voice of the Lord. That sounds like a great definition of Peter, doesn't it! Your name works the same way.

Without realizing it, I have always been able to hear the voice of the Lord. He has been speaking to me in my dreams since I was a baby. Of course, growing up I didn't know there was such a thing as being a prophet or a seer. My aunt would call me a seer but she has always been a little "out there," so I never detected the truth in her words. The Lord didn't stop there either. Because of how I felt growing up, He wanted me to know that I was always meant to be here, in my family, and that I wasn't a mistake or an accident, but part of His great plan. My older sister hates her name. She doesn't like it because she doesn't believe there is any meaning behind it. A lot of you may feel like her, but trust me there is meaning behind your name. Her name is Chiquista. She was named after the banana Chiquita. It is pronounced Cha-qui-ta. Sounds completely different than it looks, right? What looks like an accident to the naked eye is what was planned by God, and it is totally amazing. It's all right keep reading. You see that s in her name, which appears to be typo, is actually what ties me in. The last three letters in her name are my exact initials. Simone T. Allen. God knew one day that I would need to know that I was meant to be here on this earth and in this family. He knew in time, things that didn't make sense before would become clear. While she believes her name means nothing it meant a great deal to me, the second born. Her name also shows her gifts and reveals her calling. She is indeed an apostle. What is an apostle you may ask? They are part of the five-fold ministry, and are known to govern, create, generate, and pioneer. God is the apostle and we all have that gift in some way because we are of Him. However, there are people where this gift is magnified. My sister is one of them. My heart smiles while writing this because one of the many nicknames I call my sister is "The Dictator." Anyone who knows my sister knows she is very much a strong leader and a tad bit bossy. Apostles are known for breaking ground. They go and establish things. They are the FIRST to do so and follow Jesus. Jesus had twelve apostles. One of the most well-known apostles is none other than Simon Peter himself.

It doesn't stop there. As stated before, apostles were the first to follow Jesus and encounter the gifts of the Holy Spirit. My sister was the first in my immediate family to have a strong relationship with God. He chose her and separated her for the family to do so. You see, when I was eight my sister married my brother in law. He joined the navy and she moved to Virginia a few years later. Everything changed for me. I was now the oldest in the house and had to help my mom with my three youngest sisters. I started to despise my older sister. I felt she had abandoned us. To make it worse, while in Virginia she had started to become this completely new person. She became a "Bible thumper." I didn't realize that the Lord was changing her, and it was for the better. While she was getting close to Him, I found myself running from Him. Nothing made sense to me. Why would God take her and leave me to handle everything on my own? During high school, my mom got colon cancer and was extremely sick. We went from middle class to low income in a heartbeat. She was the only parent, and without her income there was none. I had to continue to grow up quickly. Often, I found myself running bank errands, speaking with collectors, making payment plans, helping my sisters with homework, hair, and dinner. My mom was the General, and I was her Colonel. To me this wasn't supposed to be my rank, it was supposed to be my sister. Why did I have to be the one to pick up the pieces? I was only in high school. Pressure and fear caused me to rebel in more ways than one. To make matters worse, my mom had married this awful man. He was verbally abusive to my younger sister and I. My life was in turmoil, and I felt my sister had left us to die.

## How to Take a Selfie

God is magnificent! He ALWAYS does what is best for us even when we don't understand. I felt abandoned by my sister but she was boldly following God and saving my life at the same time. God had pulled her first. Using her gift without even realizing it she was doing the work an apostle. When you are first to do something, the journey can be very challenging and lonely. He needed to use her to break the grounds in our family. He needed to enter us, and He used her as the door. When the time was right, He called me next in 2012. Remember THAT summer. He used her to bring me to Him so that He could save my life!

You see her name has great meaning. She is Chiquista, the firstborn child with apostolic gifting. The first called to establish a relationship with God beyond religion. She was also the first to follow Him with strong faith and is a leader in more ways than one. Much like that of Simon Peter, one of the 12 apostles of Christ.

After establishing a relationship with Him, the Lord has given me a new name. My name is still Simone, but He also calls me Redeemed Treasure. He has indeed redeemed me in more ways than one. He has established a strong foundation in me. He is now deeply rooted, and

I will never stray from Him. I am still amazed at His love for me. Despite my best efforts to run away from Him He pulled me to Him with love. Without a doubt, I know he treasures me. My past has made me strong. EVERYTHING that happened to me, He used to make me better. Because of my upbringing, I learned how to lead and follow. I have the entrepreneur spirit; I'm adventurous and love helping others. I motivate those who need an extra push. It has caused me to develop a heart for those without hope, love but more importantly those without identities. I fight for the underdogs, and no matter what, I never give up. He has shown me how to be a great parent and so much more.

You may feel like your past has no meaning but you are wrong, love. He makes beauty from our ashes. Everything you go through has meaning. You are meant to be here wherever you are. You are you and there is no one else on this planet like you. The world needs each and every one of you, and God loves us all. We are not orphans but His children. So, tell me, who are you?

Exercise time! Do you know the meaning of your name? If so, write down the meaning below. If not, Google the meaning of your name and see what you come up with. It may surprise you. Next, take a deeper look at your name and personality. Write the ways your name matches your personality and how it may be different. Both can be used to help identify your spiritual gifts. Please, when you are doing this exercise, take your time, and think outside of the box. It's going to be like playing a game of connecting the dots for sure. Look at your family, your upbringing, and other things that contribute to the person you are. I promise you everything is connected. Here are some scriptures to help with discovering your identity: John 1:12, 2 Corinthians 5:17, and Ephesians 2:8. Pray to God for guidance and let the Holy Spirit lead you.

It took years for me to understand my name. When I say years, I do mean years. I didn't understand it until 2015, and I was born in 1989. See, I told you, years! If you haven't discovered the meaning(s) of your name, don't worry, you are right on schedule. The Lord will reveal it just when the time is right.

Selfie/Dance time! Take a selfie because you are an awesome beautiful star. You are completely unique in every way and truly one of a kind. I love you guys, but He loves you so much more. Now listen to the live version of "King of Majesty" by Hillsong and Delirious. Something about that song makes me want to move. You guys will surely enjoy it. Next listen to "How He Love Us" by Kim Walker Smith. Google the lyrics, and allow the song to minister to your heart. It made me cry. Seriously it came on while I was writing the beginning of this chapter. The love of the Lord overwhelmed me so much that I stopped writing and began to thank Him. So heads up, grab a few tissues because you are going to need it. Don't say I didn't warn you!

How to Take a Selfie

Chapter 6

# The Nesting Stage: God Starts Prepping the World for You

*"Greatness has to simmer. You may have been pushing for the next level for some time, but don't worry, when it's your time it will be worth the wait and you'll make an impact near and far."*
—Lakia Robinson

There are going to be several seasons in your life where God calls you to rest in His presence. As wonderful as this may sound, it can be tough to do so. It can be hard to rest in his presence if you don't know how. In April of 2014, God called me to rest in His presence. I was working in the personal storage industry for about 5 months. The original company I worked for was the best company I had ever worked for. You could tell they cared about each employee. This was proven when my daughter Nyimah got extremely sick a week after I started working for them. She ended up having three surgeries because her condition was caught really late. God saved her. She is indeed a walking miracle. This was an extremely hard time for me and they understood. They worked around my schedule and gave me more than enough time off to be with my child. Not only that, but they allowed me to work overtime to make up the missed time. All of that without penalizing me.

Shortly after, the company sold to a bigger storage corporation and everything went downhill from there. I had become a number and the environment become toxic. The main source of this was my new manager who had previously been my coworker. She was a very broken person, and we all know: hurt people hurt people. Remember that, love. Most people who hurt us are very much hurt. Keep this in mind when dealing with them, and be sure to do your best to show them agape love. She assumed the position, but I did most of the work. She verbally abused me and tried to get me fired in every way. She started various rumors about me, and I became part of the daily gossip. Despite my best efforts to be cordial and show unconditional love, nothing seemed to get through to her. I knew deep down that something was hurting her, but I didn't know what it was. I had begun to despise her for this. Well the Lord had me to continue to pray for her. I will not lie and say that it was easy. I found myself struggling on many levels with this task. I questioned God often. Why? Why should I continue to overlook this when she continues to treat me like this? She was a senior citizen; shouldn't she know better? Why me? I didn't want to. I was being stubborn and my flesh had to be burned many times over. I mean like legit toddler stubborn. Pouty face, arms crossed, and head down. No lie. It had become hard for me to care for her at that point. One day the Lord told me to ask her why she acted the way she did. So, I boldly pulled her to the side and asked. She told me about the hurt her family had caused her growing up. How she was only close with her grandmother who had passed and she felt alone despite having three children. Sounds like someone you know? It broke my heart to hear this because I completely understood this. I asked her if I could pray for her and she agreed. We took a break, and I prayed for her. The Lord even spoke to her during the prayer through tongues. It was amazing. Later that night I had a dream. I was in the middle of this garden, but everything was dead.

## How to Take a Selfie

The weather was gloomy as if it had been raining. There was a rose bush with lots of thorns. My eyes concentrated on this one rose that was dead like everything else. Right before my eyes, it started to change. It went from grey, to pink, to bright red, and blossomed. He explained that one day she would be renewed. This made my heart smile. I was glad I had been obedient to my Father despite my feelings. Understand that you cannot operate out of feelings. Often, you will need to do the opposite of how you feel while following the Lord. Feelings aren't permanent; so do not make permanent decisions based on them! We are put on this earth to help others. Remember, what you go through is for others. Your testimony is greatly needed.

Sad to say, the woman soon went back to her old ways and the environment had become even worse than before. I no longer wanted to work there, but I felt trapped. I was a single parent, and if I had no income, we had no income. What was I to do? With tears in my eyes, I prayed to God one night. I couldn't take it anymore. The entire situation was too much. I wanted to find my purpose. I wanted to walk in my calling. I was tired of being a zombie. I wanted to live. He replied ever so sweetly, "If you follow me and have faith, I will take care of you. If you trust me on this journey, then trust that I have a plan for you. Simone are you truly ready to follow me with all of your heart?" I was ready. I knew what I had to do. The Lord was calling me to take a leap of faith and jump. It was now or never; So I decided to jump!

The next day I put in my two weeks' notice. I was going to start my own business and walk in my calling. The company did not want me leave. I left anyway. I was ready to follow the Lord even though I had no savings. None of this mattered because my mind was made up. Shortly after leaving and establishing my business, the Lord let me know that most of my time would be spent with Him. He wanted to consume my life. I had tried to make my business flourish right away. However, almost every attempt made was cancelled by the Lord. He closed doors that I should not have opened. It wasn't the season for that. It was the season of depending on Him and resting in Him. This was harder than I expected.

Exercise time! Has there been a time where God has called you to completely depend on Him? Describe your season of dependence prior to that. Name a time where God used you to speak to someone. What was your experience like? How did you react? Did you pout, like I did, or were you mature about the situation? How does God feel about us being there for others and what scriptures could we use to pray for them?

During pregnancy there comes a stage where the expecting parents began to physically prepare for the child to come. This often includes preparing the nursery, gathering much needed supplies, and baby proofing the house. It is often called the nesting stage. Well, God being the ultimate Father does the same. On the journey to finding your spiritual identity, after entering the season of dependence, the Lord begins to prepare the world for you. While you are resting in Him, He is doing all the preparations. From putting you on the minds of people you will meet in the future, to creating future opportunities for you. He is baby proofing your environment so that you will be around people who can pull your gifts out and help you learn. This is also the time that He wants you to truly learn how to love and accept yourself. There are so many moving elements, most of which you will be unaware of, just like a baby in its mother's womb. Your only job is to rest and grow. The Lord will make sure to provide all that you need.

## Simone Allen

Listen up and listen carefully. Enjoy this wonderful stage! Remember, it is okay to rest even God himself did (Genesis 2:2-3; Exodus 33:1). I didn't fully take advantage of this great gift God offered me. I often found myself trying to speed up the process because of the pressure I was feeling from the world. When I explained this journey to others including my family, many were skeptical. Obviously, it didn't make any sense for me to not only quit my job, but completely stop working for other people all together. I had two kids and no savings after all. My mom thought I was going insane. No really, she called my older sister and told her I was crazy. The only person that supported my plan was my older sister. She didn't know exactly what God was going to do, but she understood that she had no authority to question God. The fear began to set in. Did God really want me to do this? I needed advice. My sister asked me this simple question; "If you tell your children to do something and someone else tells them not to do it, do you still expect them to do it?" Of course, I would. I am their mother and would only do what I think is best for them. That's when revelation hit me like lighting. God KNOWS what's best for me. "For I know the plans I have for you, declares the Lord, plans to prosper you and not to harm you, plans to give you hope and a future." (Jeremiah 29:11. NIV).

Don't make the same mistake. Fully trust in Him. He is the best parent there is, and He would never lead you astray. Accept this wonderful gift and rest, honey bun. REST! Block out the world and its opinion. The right people will get it, and some will come around. My mother did. She fully supports His vision for my life now. It took her sometime but now that she does understand it, she is one of my biggest supporters. Honestly love, at the end of the day, if you don't follow, you will be the one who misses out. Don't be a fool. You're so much smarter than that, you super beautiful person you.

Selfie time! Imagine God's love for you. Just allow it to fill your heart beyond capacity. When you totally and whole heartily feel this, take a selfie. That picture is going to be amazing, I guarantee it. Take the rest of the day to just enjoy who you are. Get out of this book, as great as it is, and have some fun or get some much-needed rest. You deserve it.

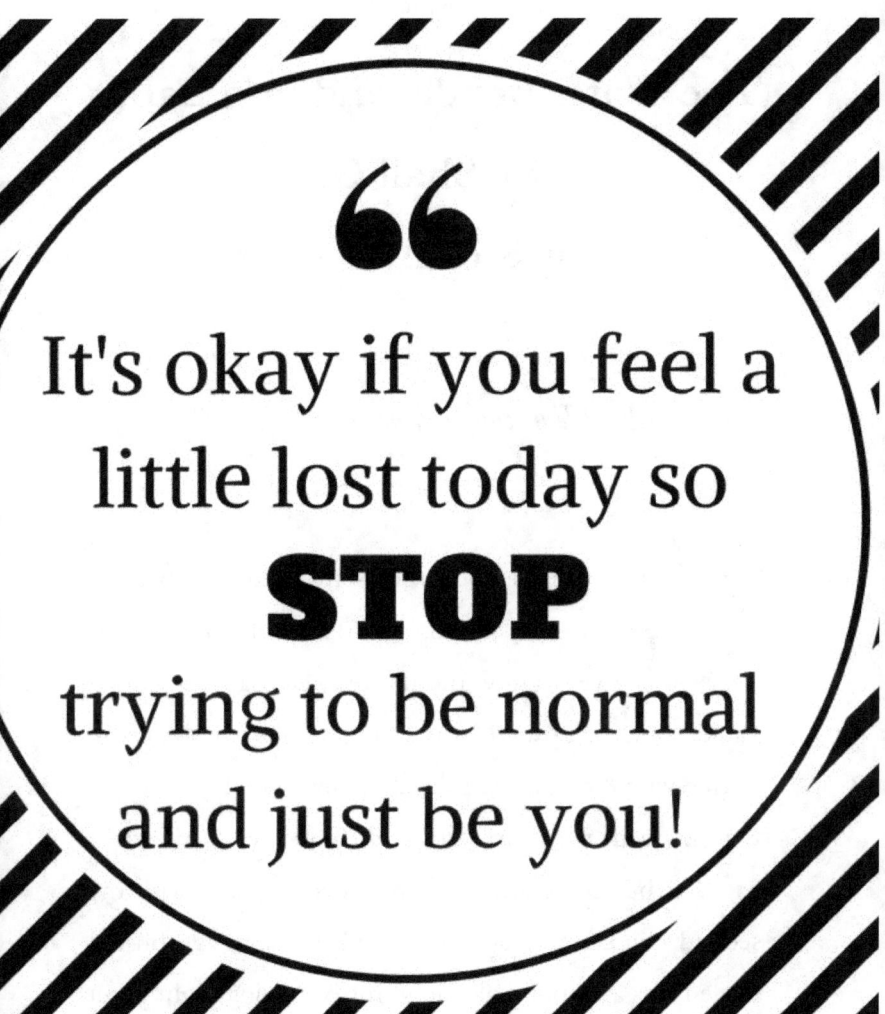

> It's okay if you feel a little lost today so **STOP** trying to be normal and just be you!

## Chapter 7

# The Water breaks and into Labor We Shall Go: The Storm Process

*"Life isn't about waiting for the storm to pass. It's about learning to dance in the Rain."*
—Vivian Greene

Growing up, you probably heard your parents share the details of your birth many times over. How mom punched dad, how dad passed out, or however the story went. It probably all started with "my water broke..." Sounds familiar? When I was pregnant with my son, I was induced; so my water bag was busted for me. When I was pregnant with my second child, my daughter, I think it may have busted while I was asleep. I woke up to my bed being slightly wet as if I had peed a tad bit. That however, could have been attributed to pregnancy bladder rather than labor.

Regardless, both started the labor process. When you began to sift into your identity you will go through a labor process yourself. There is always a brief "calm before the storm" affect similar to that of a pregnant woman's water breaking followed by a storm. A very messy trying storm! If you have seen movies or experienced child birth yourself, you know all about contractions. I have been very blessed to escape this pain during labor with both of my children. However, I have been through plenty of birthing storms, loves. Tons!

After I left my previous job at the storage facility, I went through birthing storms that strengthened me on an entirely different level. As you know, I was supposed to be resting in the Lord's presence, which I struggled with. I was trying to build a business in the season the Lord was trying to build me. Leaving my job was the water breaking. After that, the contractions came. Blow by blow, similar to labor contractions, I had to learn how to push through them. I couldn't let them knock me off my feet entirely. I needed to continue to get up. The first contraction was getting into His word.

When I left the storage company, I knew I didn't have any savings, but I knew God was great. I often told myself that God must have a great plan; He is God. You know, the King of Kings. This thought kept me positive and constantly knocked doubtful thoughts right out of my mind. Despite everyone's disapproval, I knew that somehow God would make a way. I started to get closer with God during this time. I knew He desired greatly for us to be close. He had put this intense desire for His word inside of me. This was a strange feeling because I had always hated reading the bible. I rebuked it in a way. Something about it had always seriously turned me off. Mostly because I couldn't understand it, and I struggled with reading it. This often made me feel small and insecure. Why couldn't I read this or understand it? I had always loved reading. I was a book worm to the core. No book was ever too long or complicated for me but the Bible was another story. It bored me, the words were hard to understand, and nothing made sense to me. In fact, I hated it so much that when the Bible television series came out, I constantly found myself rolling my eyes at anyone who watched it. Something was seriously wrong with this picture. One day, my sister told me of a Bible version called the Message. (It's a paraphrase not an actual translation). She told me to start with that Bible. I stared at her rudely when she told me this. No Bible was going to make any sense to me, or so I thought. I had no desire to find out anyway. Not until God placed this overbearing desire inside of me. I felt Him tugging on my heart, yearning to have a relationship. It was so deep I couldn't ignore it anymore. The Holy Spirit led me to watch the Bible television series. I could hear the voice of the Lord tell me to just try one episode. I thought it was going to be stupid and I wasn't going to like It. He pushed me to watch it anyway. Day and night I could hear Him telling me to just try it. Finally, I gave in. Not because I was interested but simply because I wanted Him to leave me alone about this matter. Trust if there is one thing I have learned about my Father is He will make you uncomfortable until you do what is asked of you. Make your life easy and just go when He says to. The next morning I watched the first episode on Netflix. It was AMAZING. Totally mind blowing. From the beginning to the end of the episode, I was completely enticed. As a total movie and book buff, I was impressed. I found myself binge watching the whole series within two days! Once I was done with the series, I couldn't wait to read the actual Bible. After all, the books were always better than the movies, right? They have so much more detail. It was time for me to order The Message. I found the book on Amazon and ordered it. It arrived within two days, thanks to Amazon Prime membership. When the mailman delivered it, I snatched it out of his hand by mistake. I was over excited to read it. I couldn't wait.

As a tradition, I wrote my name and the date that I read my very first page. I do this with all of my books. I don't exactly know why, but I have done so since I was a kid. I think it might have been to keep record of how long it takes me to read them but I don't really remember. Anywho, I started to read it. I couldn't fly through it because it wasn't made to do so. For some ironic reason, I thought I could read it within 24-hours, 48 tops because that's what I do with my books. This was not going to work with the Bible. It was way to complex. It was a book that required patience, meditating, and much more. Once I understood this, I took my time. Often times taking notes so that I could make sure I understood the content. I found myself often speaking with God and pondering Him, with an overload of questions. But dad why this? Why that? Why? Why? Why? So many thoughts ran through my mind. I had finally found a version that I could understand, and I finally had the yearning to learn the word. This however was just the beginning. The first contraction of giving birth.

Exercise time! Did you notice that when God was calling me, I naturally rebelled because of my insecurities? I made it so much more difficult than it should have been. It was difficult for me until I let go and started to trust Him. I had to push past my pain in order to get better. Much like a contraction during labor. Can you recognize your "water braking" moment? The calm before the storm? Describe your experience below. Next think about your first contraction. What was that experience like. Were you able to push through with strength or were you hardheaded and stubborn like muah? What has God tried to restore or pull out of you? How does this make you feel?

The more I found myself diving into the word, the closer I became with God. He became my dad, not just my Father. We became best friends. I became comfortable with sharing my inner most secrets with Him. The ones I kept hidden deep inside. I knew He had known them anyway, but now I had granted Him full access to my emotions. Often, I would talk to Him about nonchalant things like music, to television shows, and deeper emotions. We had daily silly faces contests, which I would always win by default because I couldn't actually see His face. Often, I would say, "Dad I totally win because I can't see you, and if you did let me see you, technically, I would have to die. So it's only right that you agree." I found myself in love with our relationship. It was calm again. That was until the second contraction hit. This one more painful than the first one. In fact, this one hurt like… well you know the saying. The second contraction was the eviction.

As previously stated I knew God was the King of Kings, and we had become closer than we had ever been my entire life. I woke up happy despite the fact the world told me to feel otherwise. I mean let's be completely honest here. I had absolutely no income whatsoever. In fact, I needed government assistance just to feed my kids. It sounds terrible doesn't it? Naturally, you make the judgment of a neglectful mom making mistakes that affected children. Trust me, every thought you're probably having right now, I have had many times over. I can assure you they were worse! Still, I had been in the presence of the Lord. I knew my pops would make a way out of no way, and He did. I mean this was all His idea. It seems like this would be an easy thing, right? Not working a traditional job and depending fully on the Lord. It's much more difficult than you think. We are tested in the fields that we need to be strengthened in. I had never completely depended on anyone in my entire life. Having to grow up fast made me a resourceful individual. I have always had the ability to figure it out, so I didn't need anyone or want to need anyone, including God. Being a dreamer, He often sent prophetic messages of the plans He had for me. One of those dreams included Him sending someone to help me financially with my rent. This person paid my rent for an entire year. That strengthened me to another level. I had faith like never before. Yes, everything was smooth sailing from there, or so I thought. I became increasingly delinquent on my rent. I would pay what I could, but it was never enough. I felt like I was in trouble. I felt tricked. I would often ask, God where this mysterious person was, and who was going to foot the bill? In the moment, I didn't understand He was trying to teach me about patience, trusting Him, walking by faith and not by sight, and much more. God always wants us to be comfortable with being uncomfortable. Like wearing skinny jeans that you can't breathe in but look amazing in. Ladies you know that feeling right? Sorry fellas, I don't know what example to use for you, so insert your own here.

I've never had a lot of financial support. There wasn't anyone I could turn to. Everyone who would help me was actually swimming in the same pond. Still, I had faith that God would keep His promise. It started small but it was growing a bit. I knew He would make a way. However, as the bills continued to pile up, my faith started to waver. I had done my best to stay positive. I had been hopeful for a long time but nothing, as far as I could see, was changing. In fact, everything appeared worst. People were praying for me, and I spoke to God daily about my concerns. My sister, Chiquista, would tell me that God was going to use my faith to show the world that He performs miracles. She encouraged me to continue on this path. While studying His word, I became familiar with the scripture 2 Corinthians 5:7, "For we walk by faith and not by sight" KJV. I knew that despite what I was seeing, God was working. Well, He was working on His own timeline and not by the world's because soon enough I was served an eviction notice.

Fear set in, but I dismissed it. God promised, and He isn't a liar. You wouldn't take my first apartment away from me would you dad? Not after you told me to go down this path. I had so many questions. My concerns grew. I couldn't allow us to get kicked out. Where would we go? I groaned and complained. Cried and prayed. I went through every emotion known to man. I felt it all. I became a bit distant and a bit bitter. I couldn't understand what was happing or why God had allowed it to get this far. This was scary, and it wasn't fun anymore. I no longer wanted to play silly face games or laugh until it hurt. I just wanted to be alone because I was hurt. I felt betrayed, like I had been tricked. I doubted God, but I doubted myself more. I told myself I must have heard wrong. That my dream wasn't a prophetic message, but a wishful dream. Simone, oh silly Simone, what a screw up you are. As it would any good parent, I can assure that it must have hurt God to hear me say these things to myself. For me to feel the way I did. For the distance to return, but He knew in time, He would make things clear to me.

Have you noticed in the movies they tell the women to breath in between the contractions? You always see people reminding them of this. I'm not sure if women actually do this in real life or not. Remember I had C-sections and was highly drugged with both kids. I had a very different experience than others. They always encourage the women to breath and it helps, right? Well, I skipped the breathing part. I couldn't calm myself and concentrate on pushing through. All I could feel was the pain. This wasn't going to happen exactly the way I saw it.

As my children and I entered court, I was hopeful that somehow, we would be rescued from the situation. Like there was going to be this big scene. The doors would swing open just as I was called and someone would walk in yelling "Stop!" The judge would look up and this person would look at me and smile. Next, they would write a check for me to my apartment complex and say something grand like "from God to you." Okay, maybe that was too grand, but you get what I mean. It was going to show the non-believers just who He was. Yes, I know, I watch way too many movies. What really happened was I was told to pay up or go. No one came to rescue us. With my head held high but my hopes low, my children and I exited the courtroom and headed home. On the way to our car a woman walking past us told me "God really loves you" and handed me a pamphlet about Jesus. I told her I know but was terribly confused. The stranger had given me hope again. Okay, He's got this, He is going to come through at the last minute and prove why He is the King of Kings. Yea, that didn't happen either. Soon enough, because no payments were made two months after receiving the eviction notice, we had to go.

Still in shock, I refused to budge. God was coming. He had to come. I needed Him to come. I couldn't pack. It was hard, and it hurt. Finally, I started to semi pack just in case He wasn't going to save us. There was still time because time is nothing to God. I was blinded and couldn't see the bigger picture. Because of this I didn't make any plans or arrangements for us to move. I was set on the miracle happening the way I wanted it to happen. My sister Chiquista got us a moving truck and helped pack. My brother and nephews helped also. I was pretty much speechless. It rained that day, but I was happy because it matched my mood. I felt God had let me down and my heart was broken.

God isn't a magical genie. You can't make a bunch of wishes and expect for them to come true. I was well aware of this but I knew that if I had faith, truly believed, and gave it my all, then God wouldn't have a problem helping me (Luke 17:6), correct? He replied, "If you have faith as small as a mustard seed, you can say to this mulberry tree, 'Be uprooted and planted in the sea,' and it will obey you." I was in a season of total dependence. He was my entire source just as He had requested. What was happening loves?

I had made it past another contraction but that one hurt, deeply. I didn't breathe through it, and I'm not sure if I pushed as hard as I could. Still, it was done and there was no going back. We had to move in with my sister and her family. They didn't have any extra rooms so the dining room was converted into a room for my children. No lie, it sucked. We were invading their space and we didn't have any.

At first, despite that the fact that it wasn't ideal, it was working. It was just a matter of time before another contraction was to come.

Selfie time! You're probably comparing my story to yours. This may have brought up some pretty intense emotions. It's ok. It's perfectly fine to feel the way you do now. However, you may be feeling, understand that it is alright. In fact, here is a hug. Of course, you have to hug yourself because I can't physically do it, but it's from me.

Now breathe in slow deep breaths, and take a selfie. Remember to totally own it.

    Eventually things started to get tense. We all bothered each other in more ways than one. I began to slip into depression, again. The negative thoughts constantly running through my mind caused panic attacks daily. I felt stuck and lost. What was my purpose? What was I supposed to be doing with my life? That year had been extremely difficult. More than difficult, it was emotionally horrible. I was losing it. I needed my own space again. I needed to be financially stable. I needed a whole list of things. This wasn't supposed to be happening, or so I thought. There was a bit of hope, though. I had this intense feeling that the next year was going to be better. That it was going to be a year of victorious breakthroughs. God was going to do great things for me. I used this to give myself hope again. I reminded myself daily that once the New Year came, so would the blessings. Well the New Year came, but things got worse. Mentally I was still suffering though. The enemy had invaded my mind. It was ugly. Plenty of times I would find myself pacing the floors severely over thinking. Feeling myself slowly deteriorating. I decided to seek help. I refused to go out without a fight and I had a desperate need to get mentally stable again.

Boldly, I admitted my problems out loud to the Lord. I could no longer attempt to hide them. I knew I needed help. I contacted my spiritual adviser. I informed her of the negative thoughts running through my mind. They were extreme and ugly. It was clear that I was struggling from depression, which included thoughts of harming myself to ease my pain. I knew that it was wrong, but the pain I felt inside felt unbearable. Immediately, my advisor began to pray for me. She went to war for me in prayer. Next, she immediately started weekly therapy sessions for me. The sessions included homework, prayer, and open conversation of why I felt the way I did. God had loved me so much that He pulled me back. All I needed to do was give it to Him and seek help.

The enemy wasn't done wreaking havoc though. He was determined to keep me in my current mental state. As you know, the enemy is against us 100%. The more you represent Christ and allow God to use you, the bigger threat you are to him, the more he is going to attack. The quicker you understand this, the less time you will waste wondering why God allows him to attack you. Remember you are a mighty weapon and your destiny will be great. Learn to be the light in the darkness. It can be challenging sometimes, but it is necessary.

Shortly after a few sessions, my car was repossessed. It was a week after the holidays and a week before my son's birthday. I cried like a baby for days. I slept for two days straight. Not just because I was sad, but also because dreaming is a stress reliever for me. I dream every time I sleep; so sometimes I go to sleep, just to ease my mind and feel better. My kids were confused. They would often ask me where the car was. Avoiding eye contact, I told them it was gone. I couldn't believe this was happening. This was supposed to be my year, but it was starting off worse than the prior year. It could have been worse when I think about it. God clearly love us. Even in sensitive situations, He is always present. The guy who repossessed my car was a fellow Christian. He allowed me to clean out my car. He knew where my vehicle was located before the start of the Holidays but waited until after, to repossess it. He tried his best to create small talk with me. Informing me of God's love, and how he always has a plan. He told me that when God takes something away, He gives us something better and that I should try to remain positive.

He was polite too. To ease the process, he offered to say that he was taking it to the shop so nosey neighbors wouldn't know exactly what was going on. The man told me He would hold it over the weekend so I could call the company and try to save my car. However, I knew I was never going to see my car again. Man, did that hurt guys! That was one big contraction. How were we supposed to get around now?

I continued with my weekly therapy sessions. They were an absolute necessity. This was NOT how I thought this year was going to be. God had different plans than I had. He wasn't done with me. I was still in labor and yes; you guessed it, soon another contraction hit.

Exercise time! God loves us unconditionally! Sometimes, this may be difficult to understand. I mean, after all, we expect Him to always cover us and never let anything bad happen. He does always cover us, but if nothing bad ever happens, how can we grow? Pain is strength. "To all who mourn in Israel, he will give a crown of beauty for ashes, a joyous blessing instead of mourning, festive praise instead of despair. In their righteousness, they will be like great oaks that the LORD has planted for his own glory." (Isaiah 61:3 NLT). The Lord will make beauty from our ashes. What you see as useless, the Lord sees as useful. Think about your journey. Think about a time when you thought God had abandoned you, but now you can see He was clearly there. I mean, what was the chance that I would receive a Christian repo man who would do his absolute best to make this as painless as possible? Of course, during the pain, I couldn't see God, but after a while when I really thought about the situation, it was clear that God was there. .Write down your thoughts about your situation. Take the time to apologize, and thank the Lord for His grace and mercy. Isn't our dad great, loves? Yep He is totally wonderful! Listen to "Who Am I" by Casting Crowns while you are writing your experience down. This powerful song reminds us of who God is! He is the King of Kings! Rejoice in His name today. Don't forget to Google it, play it, and let it marinate your soul. Love you! XOXOXO

The day had started like any other day, but tensions had been high in the house for a while now. It wasn't getting any better. Before long, my sister Chiquista and I had found ourselves in an ugly argument. Neither of us listening to the other person. Our feelings were mutual about needing to move out. I posted an ad on craigslist looking for a room. I needed to get out fast. After a lot of bazaar replies, I found a place. It seemed ideal and the owner seemed nice. I packed up and shortly after, we moved in. My family was scared about us moving in with a stranger. My mom wanted me to stay with my sister, but that was no longer an option. We had reached a point of ignoring each other so that we wouldn't tear each other's throats out. Not very Christ like at all. We were not representing well. Regardless of my mother's concern, I had given it to God.

What seemed like a positive environment in this new place was a farce. The guy had lied about his character. Let's just say, He was a wolf in sheep's clothing. He was very unhappy with himself and made it his mission to tear others down. It drove him nuts that I had an intense relationship with God. He said He had one too, but my relationship with God bothered him. Whenever I would walk around praying in tongues, he would flip out. He didn't love himself, and it was clear once you got to know him. The Lord was testing me. He wanted to see if I had matured at all and if I was learning. The man would often insult the other female roommate and myself. She was a very sweet and passive person who never stood up for. I, on the other hand, was very outspoken. I would call him out, and it drove him nuts that he couldn't control me. I don't know if it was because I have the ability to discern or because I constantly stayed in prayer, but I could see that his pain was associated with various demonic spirits. He clearly was in torment. Often I would want to let him know exactly how I felt about the way he treated people, but the Lord would always have me say spiritual uplifting messages to him instead. I was truly learning how to bite my tongue and to speak life. The Lord would remind me of Proverbs 18:21 "The tongue has the power of life and death, and those who love it will eat its fruit." He also used the song "Speak Life" by Toby Mac. I would listen to it and boogie. It helped recharged my battery, but it was hard! I won't sit here and lie, but it showed me I was stronger than I had imagined. You guys are just as strong. If you are experiencing a contraction, remember to breathe and push through it. Trust in the Lord, He knows what He's doing. As Proverbs 3:5-6 tells us, "Trust in the LORD with all your heart and lean not on your own understanding; in all your ways submit to him, and he will make your paths straight."

## How to Take a Selfie

During that time, the Lord also had my spiritual mentor bless me with a book called "The Bait of Satan" by John Bevere. This book helped change my life! It was about forgiveness. I learned I had been a very unforgiving person. It helped me to realize that I didn't even know what true forgiveness looked like or how to truly go about forgiving those who had hurt me. I highly recommend reading this book. It will pull things out of you that you didn't even know existed. With this book, I was able to learn how to forgive those who had hurt me. My sister and I also mended our relationship. Part of this was because of the book, but another part was because the loss of our cousin. Our family had lost someone who was only a month older than I am. He was murdered a week before his 26 birthday, down the street from the house we grew up in. It brought us all closer, but it hurt because we're not use to losing someone. I made a promise to God during that time that I was ready to fully walk in my calling. He had full control of my life.

While reading this book I learned why God was trying to establish a strong foundation in me. He wanted me to be deeply rooted in Him so when the storms did come, I wouldn't waver. Just as He said in Jeremiah 17:7-

8, "But blessed is the one who trusts in the LORD, whose confidence is in him. They will be like a tree planted by the water that sends out its roots by the stream. It does not fear when heat comes; its leaves are always green. It has no worries in a year of drought and never fails to bear fruit," NIV.

Isn't He astounding, loves? I wasn't going through this just for fun, but He was tearing me down to build me up. My previous foundation had been extremely faulty. Not only did He establish a solid foundation, but He also taught me what it meant to show someone agape love. Agape means Godly love. It is unconditional. It is the way God loves us and the way he desires us to love each other. However, we often offer phileo (of warmth and affection feelings) instead. It is what we show our family and friends. It is conditional, while agape love is eternal. It is forever because it is the way God loves us. I was learning how to love my fellow peer with agape love. This was difficult, but I found the more I stayed in deep prayer with the Lord, the easier it became. It was obvious that he was hurting deeply. It also showed he couldn't see the spiritual suffering or understood how to seek help for it. He never accepted any of my invitations to come to church or to learn more about God, but I continued to pray for him. He continued to bring me down and put me and my children out after a month of living there. It didn't faze me one bit. When you gain a better understanding of someone, certain things stop fazing you. You will learn that the more you seek God, the more things will become clear.

Dance/Exercise time! First Google and listen to "Your Love Never Fails" by the Newsboys. It is a great song that reminds us that God is always here for us. His love never fails! It might make you cry. It has made me cry time and again. I often feel overwhelmed by God's love for us. After you are done singing your hearts out to the Lord, it's time to do some work. Do you understand the difference between agape love and phileo love? We exhibit phileo love, but in what ways has God called you to show agape love? If you desire to love others as God loves you, then you must learn to show agape love. Ask the Lord to come into your heart on a deeper level and teach you how to show agape love. Allow the Holy Spirit to lead you. Listen to "How He Loves Us" by the David Crowder Band. Singing "Oh how he loves us, oh how He loves us, oh how he loves us. We are His portion and He is our prize." This delightful song is playing as I'm writing to you. God REALLY wants you to know this, loves. Hug yourselves twice. One from dad and one from me. Smile, because you're magnificent.

Everything we go through has a purpose. This is why we must learn to walk by faith and not by sight. I was becoming a new person in Him. It is a continued learning experience. God was using my suffering to prepare me for my future. He was showing me who I was supposed to be. I was entering my destiny. Finally, I was learning who Simone was. It was time now. I was being reborn! God tested my heart in many ways to insure I was learning. He provided many platforms for me to learn. From books and counseling to workshops and seminars. There was so much that He wanted me to know. I learned my temperaments, which finally helped me understand why I behaved the way I did. I learned my love languages, which helped me to understand how I showed and received love. He used Dr. Faith to teach me those lessons. He provided tons of resources because it was now the season for me to walk in my calling and all of them will be shared with you, love. Soon, you too shall walk into your calling. You will be reborn as well!

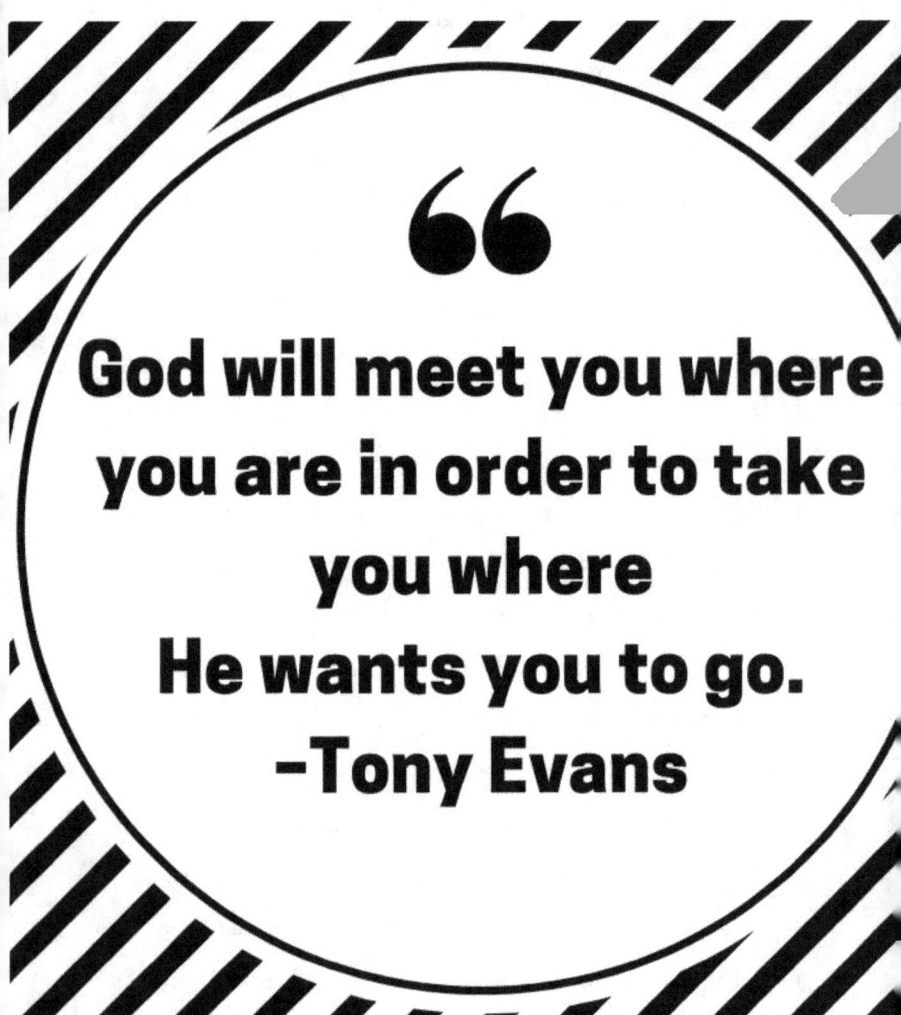

## Chapter 8

# Congratulations, You Are Born!

*"When we know and realize what we can do then we are free!"*

-Betty Blyth

You are now redeemed. No longer are you lost; no longer are you an orphan. No, you are a child of God, ripe and ready to walk in your calling. "I have been crucified with Christ. It is no longer I who live, but Christ who lives in me. And the life I now live in the flesh I live by faith in the Son of God, who loved me and gave himself for me." (Galatians 2:20 ESV)

Now that you are reborn, you will have hungry eyes and child-like curiosity. A lot of what you thought you knew will become new to you again through a different perceptive. You will gain knowledge and wisdom that can ONLY be taught by the Holy Spirit. Gifts that you didn't realize you had at the beginning of the year will start to manifest. Everything has a brand-new feel to it. Now, this isn't to say that you will live happily ever after, although in retrospect, being a child of God does in a way mean that. You will still have ups and downs. There will still be plenty of tears that will flow down your beautiful face. Even though this will still continue to happen, it won't be like before. Before you start to feel bamboozled, allow me to explain. You have been given the only tool you will ever need. God has placed a truth in you that cannot be moved. Because you are entirely armed with His love when you go through storms, you will know that they shall come to pass. You are never alone. You know for a FACT that you are a child of God, because you have accepted Jesus as your Lord and Savior and because you have been redeemed, you are indeed free. Just as He says in Galatians 5:1 "For freedom Christ has set us free; stand firm therefore, and do not submit again to a yoke of slavery." Also 2 Corinthians 3:17 "Now the Lord is the Spirit, and where the Spirit of the Lord is, there is freedom." ESV

When I was redeemed I felt different, but looked the same. On the outside, it appeared that nothing about me had changed but everything on the inside felt different. I wanted to know everything. For Him to pour everything into me so that I may soak it up like a sponge. I no longer craved the same things or wanted to be around the same people. Naturally, I separated myself from everything and everyone that wasn't aligning to His purpose for my life. Questions that I once had were answered. Not every single one but the ones He wanted to give me clarification on. My worship level was elevated. It had been upgraded because God upgraded me! In the beginning of my journey, I couldn't effectively pray or worship. I didn't know how to step into the presence of the Lord myself, so I depended on others to get me there. I didn't have a relationship with Him, and I didn't know what true love was. I was an orphan, but now, I am a child of God. This may seem repetitive but the truth is I had to be reminded of this A LOT. In fact, that lesson was repeated until I was finally able to comprehend what He was trying to tell me, that He loved me and his love was the best love there is.

When you become more like Him and changes are made, you will look different on the outside too. When I returned home to Chicago to visit my family it became clear that I no longer looked the same to people. It had really caught me off guard. People who hadn't seen me in a while, barley recognized me. My grandmother's best friend asked her several times, "was that Simone." Dazed, I wondered why she didn't recognize me, as I had known her since I was a little girl. "Mrs. Rose you don't know who I am?" I asked. Honestly, I thought it was because of old age. She was well into her eighties and her sight had become bad. My grandmother replied with a chuckle "Yes that's Simone, isn't she beautiful!" The more people I saw, including old church members and family, the more they all agreed that I looked different. The word beautiful had become like a second name for me. Beautiful? This was a long way away from the girl I once was. Naturally, the enemy tried to creep in with his doubt and hatred. He tried to play on my emotions by bringing up old wounds. Hissing in my ear statements like "so you must have been ugly before," among other insults. I had learned how to dismiss his voice by listening more to God's voice. I am beautiful now and I was then too. I've just gotten even prettier.

It sounds super cocky, right? Believe me when I tell you I thought the same thing at first. The truth is, there is nothing wrong with self -love. In fact, if you cannot love yourself you cannot love others. Let me repeat that. If you CANNOT love yourself, you CANNOT love others. In today's world, shallowness is greatly taught encourage. We believe that self-love is looking a certain way, (with the standard being magazine cover models), that being different is undesirable; We're encouraged to be anything other than who we naturally are. This creates a shell and as technology advances with the creation of more social sites, we become far less social with each other. We no longer embrace who we are; instead we mask our truths and constantly reinvent ourselves to cater to society's wants. Well, I'm sorry to tell you, but that is not living. It is an unknown death. You have officially been buried alive. Point blank, period. You cannot depend on society to make you whole. Only God can do that. Lean to Him and He will make you whole again.

When I learned to depend on the Lord, I established a relationship with Him, and I allowed Him to mend my broken heart; I became new again. The difference on the outside that people were now seeing, the reason I appeared like a completely different person to them was because I am a new person. Christ had made me new; I was made in His image just like you. My big sister pulled me to the side and told me "you have Christ on you girl, and it looks good." She was completely right! I did have Christ on me, and heck yea, this was the best fitting look ever! It had nothing to do with MY appearance really; truth is it didn't have anything to do with me. It was all about God. He got all the credit from that. #BEST TRANSFORMATION EVER

Yes, I look different, speak different, act different, and behave different. I'm still the original Simone He just upgraded me to Simone 2.0. Good news! He is going to do the same thing for you. You will act different, look different, and behave different. You are about to be brand new. Let Him upgrade you because it's totally worth it. Your old system is a no go, it no longer works for you, and it's COMPLETELY outdated. Before you start fussing love, understand that this will be a continued process every year in your life. The same way you happily upgrade your cell phone ever year is the same way God is going to upgrade you. If you camp out for a phone or jump through hoops for the latest upgrades on all of your favorite techs, you can put in the same effort for self-healing. Don't be lazy, don't complain, accept the upgrade as the wonderful gift it is. You're welcome!

# I Pledge

to try when I want to quit. To cry, scream and shout if I need to. To trust God even when my flesh doesn't want to. I pledge to run after my dreams and to explore the uncharted. To grow even when it hurts. I pledge to embrace my future and learn from my past. To be all that God has called me to be. I pledge to be ME! Uniquely ever loving rock star, Me. To dance around, laugh until my cheeks are red and eat snacks I have no business eating. I pledge to shift the world and others around me by informing them of you. To lean on you in all times and with all things. I pledge to worship you. But most importantly I pledge to be a representation of you my Heavenly Father in all things. In Jesus nameAmen#letsdothis #werock

How to Take a Selfie

Congratulations love! You made it. At this point, you have been through an extreme journey with the Lord. One that has been filled with joy, pain, confusion, hurt, love, and more. It was difficult, but you made it. To celebrate, we should dance. Oh, come on, if you have learned anything, you have learned about the art of shaking things out.

Dance time! "Let it Out" by Switchfoot is a great song to start with. I just finished listening to it, and it was simply awesome. I loved the content of the song so much that I ended up screaming. Like really, legit screaming with all of my might. As bazaar as it may sound, it was extremely therapeutic. It felt good to shake and yell out the negativity, and embrace the good. Now it's your turn. Don't you dare chicken out on me. Remember you are a total rock star who is amazing and untouchable. You are a total boss. Enjoy the song love. Get silly, let loose, and scream yourself into a better you. I love you.

XOXO, Simone Allen

Simone Allen

## **Who Child Is This?**

They look at me and ask who child is this?

With the ragged clothes and the dirt on its face.

Whose child is this they ask?

Lost and uncertain of the way

Unsure, uneasy and afraid

They look at me and ask who child is this?

That says it serves a mighty God but is poorer in economics than the average person

That dwells in poverty as its home

Who child is this they ask?

Who is hated and persecuted by the world

Outcast, taunted, and ridiculed

They look at me and ask who child is this?

## How to Take a Selfie

Without a father and with a mother who doesn't love it

Little black sheep of the family whose wool isn't beautiful or desired

Who child is this they ask?

Who sometimes doesn't have food to eat.

Scraping up loose change out of the sofa or off the street

They look at me and ask

Who child is this?

Without any authority, title nor position

That the world over looks as if it doesn't exist

They laugh and they laugh and they look at me and ask.

Who child is this?

That has been beaten and put together again

Beaten and put together again

### Simone Allen

### Beaten by all

Beaten

Who child is this they ask?

That isn't worth anything and has no monetary value

Without love and not liked

They circle me like a tornado

They mock me and throw stones

They've denied my entrance into their inner circle

They believe I will never be more than I already am.

They believe the lies

And as I began to weep a flood of tears

My Father answers, SHE IS MY CHILD

Made in my image, crafted by my hands

## How to Take a Selfie

She is my child whose value is worth more than all the gold, jewels and money in the world.

Whose value is so high that a price could never be place

Valued so much that if I was to ever lose her I would weep for eternity of her lost

Who child is this you ask?

She is my child

Who from the beginning of time I have order her steps, protected, loved and natured her

She is my child

Who has went without food of the world but has been over fed on the food of the spirit

Who you say dwells in poverty and yet she is of royalty

Who you say has not title, position

Nor authority

## Simone Allen

Any yet again she is the daughter of the King of Kings, and walks in an authority that can command a mountain to jump into the river

Never excepted into your inner circle because she has an eternal position in mines

You ask who child is this, she is MY Child!

Who you look over as unimportant

And yet she is so important to me that I know the EXACT number of hairs she has on her head.

Who is without a father but has the greatest Father there is.

I who love her so much that I gave my only begotten son to die for her so that she may have everlasting life

You look at her and ask who child is this

You mock her and beat her

And yet I have taken all of her ashes, torment and pain and given her DIVINE BEAUTY

## How to Take a Selfie

My sheep who wool is so beautiful the average eye is unable to gaze upon her

My child who I love so much I have created a buffet of food for her before her enemies

You beat her and torment her

You circle her and made her cry

But her tears are tears of joy as she worships me and dwells in my presence

She is my child I the God of Abraham, Isaac and Jacob

The God of Israel

Creator of the Heavens and the Earth

She is my child who I have perfectly crafted before time itself

Who hears my voice and knows my name

I Jehovah Jireh her provider

### Simone Allen

The Lord of all is her Father and she is forever my beloved child

They no longer look at me and ask who child is this

-Simone T. Allen

# Thank you

To my Dad, thank you for everything. From creating me to loving me. You are amazing! This entire book was written by you, and I simply typed it. You could have given up on me. You could have allowed me to stay hollow, angry, and bitter. You didn't because you are amazing. You are my best friend, and I don't have the words to describe how much I love you. Thank you for teaching me real love, for all that you do and for being you.

Jeremiah and Nyimah Allen. My lovebirds, chipmunks, kid one and kid two and two-thirds of the musketeers. Thank you for being the best kids a parent could ever want, and for teaching me how to accept agape love. God sent me you two so that He could save me. Jeremiah, keep loving others the way that you do. You have this amazing super hero talent to love others. Never change that. Nyimah, always march to your own beat, and keep your confidence. Your super power is knowing who you are and being comfortable in your own skin. One day God will use you two to change the world, ready yourselves.

Chiquista. I used your real name because I know that you want your "thank you" to be super dignified. *clears throat*. My darling sister, thank you (by the way you need to read this in a British accent for the full affect) for always being there for me. You are not just my sister, but also my annoying friend. You taught me how to be okay with starting my journey with the Lord. He uses you to help keep me on track, because we all know I like to go all over. No matter what dream I chase, you're always on board because you trust me to be me. Thank you for letting me be great. (Finally)

My little sisters, Leashia Jr., Tatiana, and Miracle: Thank you for teaching me how to protect and care for others before I had kids. You guys were literally my test kids. Baby, despite our many fights, you have always been in my corner. You don't agree with my choices but if I need you, you are there. I have ALWAYS admired your ability to live your life on your own terms. I love that the most about you. That and the fact that you graduated from college first, you're always down for reckless adventure, and you are my Kel. (You know Kel from Keenen and Kel). Never forget, you are and forever will be the other sister. Tatiana, I will never forget the many times you would sneak into my room to take the babies so I could sleep. The times I would come home from work to my room being thoroughly clean. You have always been such a big help to my kids and me, and I cannot thank you enough. Stay dancing Tati. Seriously, you have such a big heart. Don't hide it. Share it with the world. Finally, Miracle, my raging bull. Out of all of us, you are the one who is literally always ready for a fight. You're the true definition of fearless! One day the world will be listening to your music or reading your books. When that time comes, the Earth will never be the same. I love you guys.

My sweet Ollie Allen. I love you more than you will ever know. You taught me how to count, how to tie my shoes, and how to make the best banana pudding EVER! You were there at my choir recitals, you placed me in plays, you fed me and loved me. Thank you for being the heartbeat of our family and the best grandmother in the world. I hope I've made you proud granny!

To my nieces and nephews. Michael, Kai'von, Paris, Alexander, and Zionna. I love you guys. Michael, as annoying as you are and yes, you annoy me, I know that the Lord is going to use you for something unimaginable.

Kai, if you ever feel misunderstood or alone remember, I will always have your back. The NBA won't be ready for the sequel (PS: you will lose that bet). Paris, although you talk my ear off, I love you. Stay fabulous, helpful, and an entrepreneur. #blackgirlmagic. Zi zi, your little cute self. You are hilarious! Your laughter lights up a room. Use it to shine light on dark situations.

Old man, you know who you are but just in case, yes Michael; I'm talking to you. Originally when you married my sister, I didn't like you. Now that I think about it, I'm not convinced I like you now. I'm just joking with you. To be honest though, I have six biological brothers on my dad's side, but you are the only brother I have ever known. You have been in my life since I was six. Got on my nerves, nagged, and made me cry just like a brother would. Our relationship has grown a lot. Thanks for everything OLD MANNNNNN. (Say man slowly like it's fading away for a more dramatic affect.)

Finally, to my mom, Leashia D. Allen Sr. Hey girl hey. Knowing you, you're irritated that I did you last. You probably skipped over everyone else's thank you section, except for granny's, to get straight to yours. You probably also assumed I would put you next to granny. Wrong lady, so wrong. I put you last because I like messing with you and because I LOVE you. There were times when I thought you pushed me to far and made me grow up to fast. However, I know now that you were preparing me for my destiny. You are an amazing mom. I don't say it enough but you really are. You have instilled entrepreneurship, hustle, and culture in me. There are so many sacrifices you made for me to become the woman I am today. Thank you for raising me mom. Thank you for pushing me mom, and thank you for growing with me. You are the absolute best mom, and I am glad God chose you!

Thank you to every person who has ever been there for me. My longtime friend La'Vonna who knows me like no other. Adrienne, my spiritual sister for always going to war for me. Elder Shanel and Pastor Gail for both guiding me and being my spiritual advisors during my babe season in Christ. You both have done so much for me. The Barrons for taking us into your home. You guys are awesome. To Cornerstone Worship Center, thank you for teaching me the difference between relationship and religion and opening my eyes to praise and worship to the Lord. I sincerely thank you all.

To my readers, thank you for reading my book, being fabulous, and for being brave. Your support is amazing!

To my publisher thank you for taking a chance on me. Tiheasha, from our first conversation I knew that you understood my vision. You could have said no, but you said yes. Thanks for publishing my first book.

Sincerely,
Simone T. Allen

## Additional songs

Greater by Mercyme

Beautiful by Phil Wickham

Multiplied Needtobreath

Times by Ten North Avenue

Fix My Eyes by for King & Country

The Hurt & The Healer by Mercyme

There Will be a Day by Jeremy Camp

Fall Apart by Jason Wilson

Closer by Shawn McDonald

Broken Hallelujah by The Afters

King and Queens by Audio Adrenaline

Let it Out by Switchfoot

Beautiful by Mercyme

Fill me up by Casey J

Spirit break out by Kim Walker Smith

The Only Name by Big Daddy Weave

Made a Way by Travis Green

Every Good Thing by The Afters

My God is Awesome by Charles Jenkins

Better by Jessica Reedy

Unstoppable Love by Jesus Culture featuring Kim Walker Smith

You Love Me Anyway by Sidewalk Prophets

Best Day of My Life by American Authors

Different Light by Big Daddy Weave

Victory by Tye Tribbett & GA

Intentional by Travis Greene

# From Ashes to Beauty:

## A 365 Self-love Selfie Challenge.

**…and provide for those who grieve in Zion-- to bestow on them a crown of beauty instead of ashes, the oil of joy instead of mourning, and a garment of praise instead of a spirit of despair. They will be called oaks of righteousness, a planting of the LORD for the display of his splendor.**

**Isaiah 61:3**

Okay my lovelies; it's time to continue our journey. In the beginning of this book, I told you that you would have to do a selfie challenge for a year. That's right, EVERY day I want you to take a picture. Doesn't matter how you look or feel. The purpose is to create documentation of your journey. Sometimes it's hard for us to see our growth. Creating a picture journal will allow us to capture our feelings. It's also something that can become a family heirloom. A way to share a tool you used to document your journey of finding your identity in Christ. It really is a simple process. Take a picture every day. That's it, loves! I promise you, if you commit to the process, you will be blown away with the results. Be sure to share your photos on Instagram, and tag me so that I can view your journey with you. I look forward to seeing your beautiful faces!

    Love you,
    Simone Allen

www.ingramcontent.com/pod-product-compliance
Lightning Source LLC
Chambersburg PA
CBHW050540300426
44113CB00012B/2192